WHAT THEY SAID

---

25 YEARS OF TELLING STORIES

Michael DeMasi

Front cover and back cover designed by Mike DeSocio [with assistance from Melissa Mangini] Back cover top photo: Michael DeMasi interviews Evan Blum inside the former Central Warehouse cold storage building in Albany. By Donna Abbott-Vlahos, courtesy of *Albany Business Review*
Back cover bottom photo by Mike DeSocio

Printed in the United States of America
The Troy Book Makers · Troy, New York · thetroybookmakers.com

To order additional copies visit michaeldemasi.com or shoptbmbooks.com

ISBN: 978-1-61468-474-9

For Emma and Sophia

CONTENTS

PREFACE

———

There are two reasons I decided to publish a collection of stories I've written as a journalist.

The first is for my twin 9-year-old daughters, Emma and Sophia. They know dad works as a reporter, and they've seen my picture in the newspaper, but they know nothing about the stories I wrote long before they were born or most that came afterward. Consider this a time capsule of sorts they will hopefully open someday and learn about some of the people I've met.

The other reason is many of these stories aren't easily found in an electronic database. Searching through microfilm at the library is becoming a lost art. While it's true millions of old newspaper articles are archived online, finding what you're looking for can be tricky.

This book, then, is a way to preserve and share some of my favorite work.

By my rough calculation, I've had about 10,000 bylines since my first newspaper article in high school. I'm proud of my work but the vast majority of those stories are utterly forgettable.

Covering local government in small cities and towns, as I did for many years, produces a mind-numbing amount of process news: "The planning board tonight will consider a request by a developer to build 36 single-family homes on land that was once a strawberry farm." It's important to residents who live near the old farm and don't want anyone else invading their suburban paradise. Otherwise, it was just another 300 words slapped on a page inside the "B" section.

"Filling the hole," is the expression among grizzled reporters, a reference to the space around advertisements called the news hole. The joke is that editors care about filling the hole every day, and nothing else. [For the record, at age 49, I'm only semi-grizzled].

In researching this book, I encountered plenty of those stories. So many, it's a wonder I found enough worthy of reprinting. Less than 100 were truly memorable. From there, the list was narrowed further. I settled on 40 — a nice round number.

The people you'll meet on these pages include a priest at a maximum security prison in upstate New York who grew up on a farm in Ireland; a genial clock enthusiast whose real name was Smiley Lumpkin; a man who fled the Communist regime in Hungary and won a taxi medallion in Albany by playing a game of bridge; and a home foreclosure specialist who says her large, extended family puts the 'fun' in dysfunctional.

A series of stories explains why hundreds of Guyanese moved in the 1990s from New York City to Schenectady, and the suspicions and resentment that followed. In another article, a woman is haunted by what happened to her husband after he died in a state prison.

One story tells the tale of a man who dressed like a police officer and drove around town serving eviction notices, but isn't a cop. There's also a wealthy socialite who dressed as Cinderella on Halloween and handed out candy bars, including a dozen with a $100 bill tucked inside.

Other stories are personal: the battle against a woodchuck living under my backyard shed; rushing into the basement with our children when a tornado warning flashed on my phone; the sublime joy of sleeping in a tent on a summer night; the surprise of being reunited with my wallet after it spent more than three years locked in a supermarket safe.

The last story in this collection is about my great friend and mentor, Marv Cermak, one of the best storytellers I've known. He didn't mince words in person or print.

The articles I picked reflect the fullness of life and the variety of people. There is heartache and joy, honor and misdeed. I dedicated this book to my young daughters. There are many stories I look forward to sharing with them, but it's not a children's book. Some of the content is more appropriate for when they are older.

All of the articles were published between 1992 and 2017 at three upstate New York newspapers: *The Post-Star* in Glens Falls, *The Daily Gazette* in Schenectady, and the *Albany Business Review*. Each gave me permission to reprint the stories and photographs.

Changes were made to correct typos, tighten up sentences or add details that weren't included in the original versions. I also rewrote some headlines. I've had great editors over the years. They rescued me many times. Still, some things slipped passed us.

Compiling these stories also gave me the opportunity to follow up on the people I've written about. There are brief summaries of what happened to many of them throughout the book. Several have died. With others, our conversations picked up from where we left off years ago.

Except for four years at Ithaca College, I've spent my life living and working within an hour's drive of where I was born and raised: Troy, New York, an old industrial city on the Hudson River just north of Albany, the state capital. I never really yearned to move elsewhere. There were cover letters and resumes sent for job openings in other states when I was nearing graduation but it would have been tough to accept any offers.

As the youngest of four children, I felt a responsibility to be near my parents, who were both in their 60s when I was in my 20s.

They came to the United States on July 15, 1963 with my brother, Ralph, who was 6, and sister, Nell, 4, from the small town of Gioiosa Ionica [Jay-osa Yoh-naka] in the Calabria region of Italy, at the tip of the boot. My sister, Judy, was born less than two years after they settled in Troy. I was born in 1969.

My father was a master tailor. My mother was a dressmaker. America offered the promise of better pay to support their children. It's an understatement to say leaving behind their family, friends and lifestyle was a tremendous sacrifice. I couldn't imagine packing up my wife and two kids, saying goodbye to everyone we know and moving with little money to a foreign country where we don't speak the language.

Like scores of other immigrants, my parents had to learn English. Some of my earliest memories are of my father reading the newspaper, a habit he brought from the old country. His daily routine made an impression on me.

My parents learned to speak English remarkably well considering they had no formal instruction.

Contrast that with my experience, an American kid who spoke English from day one, heard Italian spoken at home and took Italian classes in high school. Yet, I've only mastered "Yes," "good," "thank you," "Merry Christmas" and a few other conversational basics. My attempt to talk with relatives in Italian turns into light comedy as I mangle words.

Growing up in a home with parents who spoke with an accent you become aware of how exasperating it felt for them to not always be understood. I remember making phone calls on my parents' behalf to the utility company to ask about the charge on a bill or some other matter. Getting thrust into this role as a teenager teaches you the power of language and how not to be intimidated when asking questions.

I remember visiting relatives in Connecticut, riding along with my Uncle Lou as he did errands in the town where he lived with my Aunt Teresa. Uncle Lou, a blue-collar guy, would routinely ask, "How's business?" when handing over money to the cashier. It's a simple but effective question.

I remember sitting at home in front of a typewriter, frustrated I had to look at the keys to type correctly even though my sister Nell didn't have to peek. She was taking a typing class in high school. I was in elementary school.

Looking back, these experiences help connect the dots to understand my interest and skills in newspaper reporting.

It certainly wasn't a job I envisioned or could comprehend when I took a journalism class in my junior year of high school with a teacher named Jo-Ann Coyle. After completing one of our first assignments Mrs. Coyle told me, "You have a knack for this." That confidence boost propelled me to join the student paper.

We barely knew what we were doing but knew enough to put out a fairly regular edition of *The Challenger*. If nothing else, it taught me about deadlines, teamwork and the fundamentals of publishing. In college I spent the first two years pursuing broadcast journalism before realizing I didn't like being on camera. Plus, I missed writing.

Ithaca College was also the place where I met my future wife, Lori, who was a year ahead of me in the School of Communications. She owned a car; I didn't. The relationship we formed during rides to and from home — she lived in Ballston Spa near Troy — blossomed years later into love. If you saw the movie "When Harry Met Sally" that's basically our story. We got married in October 2000 and I was welcomed into the family by Lori's parents, Tom and Fran Mithen, and her brother, Dave.

God has blessed me with caring, supportive family and friends throughout my life.

My junior and senior years in college formed the basis of what became my career path. I liked working as a reporter at *The Ithacan*: chasing stories about topics that interested me; interviewing students, faculty and staff; seeing my byline. In my senior year, our student advisor, Paul Heaton, told us about salary data the college must disclose to the Internal Revenue Service.

The result was a story that focused on the college president receiving a 20 percent raise in the same year that faculty got an average raise of 5 percent. Six senior administrators, whose salaries were controlled solely by the president, received an average raise of 9.8 percent. The increase for the sole female administrator was 1.8 percent.

It was a straightforward, by-the-numbers type of story with comments from the board of trustees and a faculty representative but not from the college president, J.J. Whalen. He didn't make himself available for an interview.

The story made a bigger splash after a freelancer at *The Post-Standard* in Syracuse, who was also an Ithaca College student, wrote a front-page story about our story under the headline, "Ithaca College Sheds Secret."

The reporter, Meg Green, took a different tack, writing that student journalists "blew the lid off one of the most closely guarded secrets" at the college — the size of Whalen's salary. The amount, $213,125, was more than twice the median salary of college presidents in the U.S., she reported. She also had some fiery quotes from angry professors.

The underlying theme was good [underpaid faculty, muckraking journalists] vs. evil [powerful men, greedy institution]. The Associated Press ran with the story and it appeared in newspapers across New York. This was long before the internet made it routine to instantly share and see articles from everywhere. Getting picked up by the AP was a big deal. It meant a story had impact and would be read by a much larger audience.

The attention was an adrenaline rush, though I was dismayed to see the story portrayed differently from the way I had reported it. I even wrote a short column in *The Ithacan* bemoaning how it was playing out, accusing the media of sensationalism. In hindsight I sound sanctimonious. Two weeks later, professors and students were marching to the administration building on campus to protest Whalen's salary and demand pay equity. I never expected my reporting to provoke anyone to take action. It was a valuable lesson about the power of the press.

After graduation I spent a month touring Italy and visiting relatives [my grasp of the language improved by the end of the trip but quickly faded]. Along the way I convinced myself going to work at a newspaper would be a financial dead end. The pay in journalism is miserly, and I had wracked up thousands of dollars in student debt. The best option, I reasoned, was to get a job in public relations but there weren't many opportunities for students right out of college.

Fortunately I didn't give up on newspapers. Editors across the state received my cover letter, resume and story clips. The manila envelopes wound up at the bottom of a thick pile because nobody was hiring. The country had slipped into a recession when oil prices shot up after the Persian Gulf War ended. Students in the class of 1991 were handed diplomas and walked into the bleakest employment market in a decade.

I did what so many others had to do: take any job I could. I went back to work at a pub in downtown Troy where I had been a waiter for several years while home on school breaks.

One night, while learning the basics of bartending, I met Susan Graves, who happened to be the editor of a local weekly paper, *The Spotlight*. She needed a freelancer to help write a special edition focused on small businesses. I jumped at the chance. It was one of those right-place, right-time moments that wound up opening many other doors.

More than 25 years later, I've been fortunate to continue doing a job I love in an era of economic and technologic upheaval in the news media business.

My features editor at *The Post-Star* memorably asked in the early 1990s, "Why do we need email when we can just pick up the phone and call someone?" Fast-forward to today. Exclusive stories are no longer broken on tomorrow's front page. They are this moment's tweet. Readers are the big winners in this transformation but scores of reporters and editors lost their jobs because the fat profit margins that publishers once enjoyed have shriveled.

I've survived and adapted to the changes. I've also learned a lot about reporting, writing and people. After all these years, I'm still learning. It's one of the most rewarding parts of the job.

Despite the public's low opinion of the press, and bogus accusations of "fake news," the words "I'm a reporter" still carry weight. They can break down the walls surrounding personal and professional lives. They can expose ugly truths and spark reform. The work reporters do is vitally important to a healthy, functioning democracy — especially now.

Journalists must be attentive listeners and question their assumptions. They have a duty to hold the powerful accountable and to admit their own mistakes. They must be honest with their sources.

They should take their jobs seriously, but not themselves.

They have to accept the fact much of what they write won't make waves. We are drowning in an ocean of content. Screens large and small distract us on demand.

By the time Emma and Sophia are adults, news published on dead trees may be a quaint memory of a bygone era. But timely, accurate information will still be essential to understanding the world.

I can picture the girls telling their children, "We remember when your grandfather would sit reading the paper."

If you made it this far, hopefully you'll find time to turn the page and read the words that follow.

MEN
AT
WORK

MINISTRY BEHIND BARS

December 20, 1992

The Post-Star

"My God, how did I go from a quiet farm in Ireland to one of the toughest prisons in New York state?"

The question that dawned suddenly on the Rev. Jim Hayes made him pause for a moment. Inside the prison cafeteria, the clank of silverware and chatter of guards seemed to be far off somewhere as he pondered the answer. It was a rare time of near-solitude.

Very soon he would parcel out the pieces of his day like a waiter trying to serve a room full of hungry people. At Great Meadow Correctional Facility, a maximum-security prison in the Washington County town of Comstock, there are usually more people to see and more things to do in a day than the clock allows.

The frustrations of 14 years on the job don't show on his face. Even on this day, when things got to be their most hectic, Hayes didn't lose his temper. He just took a breath, looked straight ahead and went about his business.

Tall and broad-shouldered, Hayes has a think Irish accent that adds an edge to his presence, a kind of street-smart toughness prisoners can respect.

In the morning, when he spoke briefly to a group of new arrivals, his voice commanded the small room. Very precisely, he explained the religious services offered at the prison and how important it was to fill out the family information questionnaire.

"I feel for a person that's denied a funeral trip because we can't prove a family relationship," he said.

The fresh inmates, an absent look on their faces, listened quietly.

When the talk was over, Hayes turned and walked out the door. Upstairs in his

The Rev. Jim Hayes
[Photo by Michael DeMasi, courtesy of *The Post-Star*]

office, he set about his daily tasks. Prisoners who requested call-outs came to see him. He was on the phone with administrators trying to straighten out a problem with the meals prepared for the Buddhists. He had to sign a paper so an inmate could use a tape player.

As senior chaplain he's part counselor, part administrator and part spiritual leader. Along with a full-time Protestant minister, full-time imam and part-time rabbi, he attends to the needs of more than 1,500 prisoners, about one-third of whom are registered as Catholics.

In some ways, he said, it's like being pastor to a neighborhood church. In here, though, the basket isn't passed for collections and the Communion wine isn't kept at the back of the chapel.

This day, Hayes held a special service for the Feast of the Immaculate Conception, a holy day of obligation for Catholics. The prison chapel is a room with rows of chairs and permanent altar at one end. Paintings on the walls depict the Stations of the Cross.

By 8:50 a.m., the chapel was alive with activity. In one corner a five-piece band made up of inmates played spirited jazz. Missalettes and choir books sat on the chairs. Inmates wearing either red or green shirts filled the room and greeted their friends with hugs and handshakes. Some sat alone quietly. Others talked.

Most were men in their 20s and older, either black or Hispanic. A few noticed the reporter in the back row. They were polite, for the most part. One even acted as a kind of tour guide, explaining the church service and why it was important to the inmates.

"When you get here, it gives you more time to focus on things you took for granted on the streets, like church," said Michael Garcia, a 23-year-old who's been in prison five years.

Garcia sat next to the table with the Communion gifts. Like many in the room, he's a regular at the services. Throughout the Mass, most of the inmates remained quiet and respectful. Those who did talk weren't unruly. Except for the homily, the Mass is said in both English and Spanish.

At the end of the service, one prisoner stood up suddenly to address the others. With arms waving nervously in the air and his voice cracking, he expressed how grateful the Puerto Rican inmates were for the special Mass held the week before in celebration of St. Barbara.

He gave thanks for those who attended and who "gave their hearts to God." Above all, he said, he gave thanks to Hayes for sanctioning the Mass.

The entire room clapped when he finished speaking.

Along two sides of the room, large windows let in the early sunlight. With a turn of the head, the tranquility of the chapel was broken by the watchtowers looming outside.

Born and ordained in Ireland, Hayes came to America in 1966. He learned about counseling and social work at Siena College in Loudonville. He taught in the church school at St. Helen's in Schenectady. In Cohoes he was director of religious education for five years.

When word came the state was looking for a priest at Great Meadow, he applied. At age 38 he became the prison chaplain.

"I had this on my mind since my college days," Hayes said.

It was either the prison ministry or the military, he figured. Both have a lot of structure and regimen.

Now 52, Hayes seems to have been a perfect fit for the job. Caught between the rules and regulations of the administration and the needs of inmates, he learned to walk a fine line between both.

"You have to be very conscious of the needs of the other units," he said, referring to the guards, teachers and hospital staff. "You become a part of a team. You're not a Lone Ranger."

At the same time, he's made certain prisoners don't see him as a "priest in blue," someone who's just a front for the guards and warden.

"If I'm walking down the corridor and see inmates and officers," he said, "I say hello to all."

He never asks prisoners about the crime they committed. All he needs to know, he said, is how much time they're doing. He also doesn't show any favoritism for the Catholics. His door is open to anyone.

"Our philosophy is, when a person needs help, it doesn't make a difference what [religion] he is," he said.

As senior chaplain, he must notify inmates when there's been a death in the family. This is hardest when it's an unexpected death, he said, because the inmate is called out of his cell and escorted to the office by a guard.

"They know when they're being brought up here I don't have good news," he said.

He's seen inmates go running from his office, screaming uncontrollably. Others have punched the wall in outrage.

He's also on call for emergencies. To date, his worst experience was the night 12 years ago when an inmate barricaded himself in a cell and started slitting his body with a razor blade. For nearly 20 minutes, Hayes tried in vain to get the man to hand over the razor.

"He got a letter from his wife," Hayes explained. "She didn't want anything to do with him. He was covered in blood. He said he was going to end it all."

Hayes, who had never met the inmate before, eventually calmed him down. When the prisoner was taken to the infirmary, the doctor asked Hayes to help with the stitches.

"That's an incident that will always remain with me," he said.

Although the constant demands wear him down on occasion, he seems to draw strength from it all. During holidays, when depressed inmates often hit their lowest point, he spends much of the day at the prison to counsel and meet with them.

"This is where I really feel I belong," he said. "It's a tough time for them."

Many new prisoners like to make a bargain with God. The deal usually works something like this: "God, I will pray every day and promise to change my ways if I can just get out on my appeal."

For the first couple months, Hayes said, he sees inmates who come to the weekly Mass regularly. Then, after they lose the appeal, they drop out of sight.

"I see it happen quite a bit," he said. "You try to prepare them not to get their hopes up too high."

It's difficult, though, especially for those new to the system. Some think going to church can help their parole records, or that Hayes will "put in the good word" for them. When there's a special religious program, they ask for a certificate proving they attended.

"Some come because they feel the church provides the only normalcy in a crazy house," he said. "At least for an hour, they feel like they're in a good place, a safe place."

Sunday morning Mass is standing-room-only as more than 100 inmates crowd into the small chapel. Many also take part in the religious programs at night.

Despite all the doubts about a prisoner's sincerity, Hayes believes jailhouse conversions can be legitimate. When everything else has collapsed around a person, sometimes religion is the only structure left.

"With some, they've suddenly realized their life has been nothing but hell," he said. "They finally wake up and say this isn't how I'm gonna live."

Admittedly, that's a small percentage of the population. For those who truly do make a change, though, Hayes sees some payoff in the end.

"They try to find [God] in themselves," he said. "I hope they would build on that."

Walking out of the cafeteria that afternoon, a guard told Hayes he would be bringing up an inmate who needed to call his family.

As he headed down the hallway to his office, a staff member stopped Hayes and dumped some paperwork on him. Inside his office an inmate came to complain the guards wouldn't let him out of his cell despite being on the call-out list.

Hayes seemed to breeze through it all, juggling his schedule in his head and trying to find time for everything. He made a phone call to change his afternoon appointment. He asked an inmate to collate some papers. He greeted the rabbi who dropped by to say hello.

And the question of how he went from a small farm in Ireland to one of the toughest prisons in New York didn't seem to cross his mind.

*   *   *

The Rev. James Hayes was 63 years old when he died on November 13, 2004 at Glens Falls Hospital after a short illness.

"To acknowledge or even list the committees or the groups of people that Jim has worked with or on behalf of is an immeasurable task," his family wrote in the obit.

In lieu of flowers, they suggested donations be given in his memory to local soup kitchens and food pantries.

Father Jim, as he was known, was "a model of compassion, humility and love," wrote Michael Miller of Niskayuna in an online guest book. "He loved justice. He lifted up the lowly."

Linda Benoit Ellingsworth of Queensbury was a student at Keveny Memorial Academy, a Catholic school in Cohoes, when Hayes started teaching there in 1969.

"He expanded our young minds by challenging us to study the world's other religions," she remembered. "His later work with inmates at Great Meadow showed the depth of his commitment to humanity."

TRUCKER GROWS AT FAST AND FURIOUS PACE

June 18, 2007

Albany Business Review

In the first few minutes you meet Joe Champagne, you'll learn he's an eighth-grade dropout who owns a fast-growing waste-hauling company that was bankrolled by his good friend, a cattle farmer from Batavia.

"I'm loud and I'm proud," Champagne will tell you, flexing his beefy biceps. "I'm a big, bad boy."

Spend a little more time and you'll see through the exterior of a tough guy who was once shot at while watching TV in the living room of his home in Schodack.

The motive for the shooting is unknown, but Champagne believes it was related to his business, Champagne Carriers Inc., at the Port of Albany.

He wasn't hurt. The shooter, who fired four or five rounds from outside the home on the night of Oct. 3, 2005, was never caught, according to State Police Senior Investigator Deborah Komar.

Champagne, 46, cares deeply about his company and carrying on a family trucking legacy that began with his grandfather's home heating oil business in Rensselaer, Champagne Oil Co.

"I take this business seriously," he said. "This is all I have in life. This is my reason for breathing."

In less than two years, Champagne has acquired a fleet of 60 "walking floor" tractor-trailers. The specially designed trucks haul tons of garbage from downstate transfer stations to Seneca Meadows in western New York and other landfills. There, the waste spills onto the ground through moving slats on the floor.

After dropping the load, drivers return the empty trailers to Albany. The next day, the cycle starts again.

His drivers log 500 miles or more each shift. His diesel fuel bill runs about $10,000 a day.

"Joey takes a personal approach," said Rocky LaRocca, business development director at Seneca Meadows in Genesee County. "He goes out and meets each one of his potential customers individually, explains his services and either closes the deal or moves on."

Last year, Champagne Carriers had $6.8 million in revenue [Champagne used a yellow marker to highlight the amount on his federal income tax return]. Profit margins are slim in the industry, he said, averaging 3 percent to 5 percent.

His trailers are easy to spot on the Thruway. They're the ones with CHAMPAGNE painted in white letters, flanked by two glasses of champagne. The tractor engines are numbered by pool balls and playing cards painted on the side of the hoods. The No. 18 truck, for instance, is a 10 of spades and eight of diamonds.

Why would the owner of a transfer station in the New York City region hire Champagne? It comes down to persistence and service, he said.

Champagne squeezes his burly frame into the driver's seat of his black Cadillac Escalade and visits places he said most men wouldn't dare go.

"I say, 'Hey, I'm Joey Champagne. Is Frank here? Is Carmine here? Is Vinny here?'" he said. "I don't walk in like a sissy ... like a petunia. I walk in like I'm supposed to be there and I get seen, not just heard. And I usually leave with work."

Joe Champagne
[Photo by Donna Abbott-Vlahos, courtesy of *Albany Business Review*]

He wants his company to grow bigger. He has filed papers to start a demolition company and do household waste pickup in Rensselaer County, where he would compete with County Waste, Allied Waste Services and other haulers.

Gil Houk, an official at County Waste in Clifton Park, wasn't too familiar with Champagne Carriers and wasn't concerned about another hauler popping up.

"There's a lot of competition around," Houk said.

Champagne spent 16 years as a driver and dispatcher for his older brother, Billy, who owned Champagne Contracting, which had more than 100 tractor-trailers hauling waste. Billy Champagne was diagnosed with lung cancer in 2003 and tried to find a buyer for the company.

Joe Champagne didn't have the money but turned to his friend, Bill Baskin, for help.

Baskin raises cattle in Batavia in Genesee County. Together, they offered $4 million for the business. Champagne said they were outbid $1 million by R. J. Valente, a big gravel company in Rensselaer County.

His brother sold to Valente.

The decision crushed Champagne.

"I had a heart attack and almost died the next day," Champagne said. "My brother died four months later."

Champagne recovered from the heart attack, sold his house and moved with his wife, Kim, to Florida. Several months later, he heard that deliveries to Seneca Meadows had declined since Valente took over the routes. LaRocca, the official at Seneca Meadows, confirms this. Valente didn't return a call seeking comment.

Sensing an opportunity, Champagne said he flew up from Florida to meet with officials at Seneca Meadows and with his friend, Baskin. Baskin offered to financially back Champagne. On May 13, 2005, Champagne went into business for himself as a waste-hauling company in Schodack.

Within a year and a half, the company grew so much he needed more space. He was able to get a good deal on a garage and storage yard at the Port of Albany and moved there in October 2006.

"My feeling is, he's a hard-working individual that will do whatever it takes to get the job done," said Terry Hurley, chief financial officer of the Albany Port District Commission. "He's a stand-up guy."

When he's not on the road trying to sign up more clients, Champagne can be found in his cramped office at the port. A half-dozen calendars are on one wall, each turned to June 2007 [they were gifts from clients and vendors; he felt he couldn't say no].

A peg board behind his desk holds keys and a baby pacifier, an inside joke between him and his wife that he runs a day care center, not a trucking business.

"My office door is never closed to anyone," he said. "If you have a problem, come see me. The secret is to take a half-bad employee, find out what's wrong in his life and turn him around and make him a good employee."

*   *   *

Champagne Carriers Inc. is no longer in business at the Port of Albany. I tried to contact Joe Champagne to find out what happened, but had no success.

At some point he started a different company, Champagne Demolition LLC, in an industrial area near the port.

The company ran into trouble when the U.S. Department of Labor accused Champagne of firing an employee in 2010 who had reported asbestos was improperly removed at a school in Gloversville.

The federal government sued in 2012, claiming Champagne had violated the employee's whistleblower rights, and the case wound its way through the courts.

In December 2017, Champagne Demolition and Joe Champagne were ordered to pay the worker $173,793 in back wages, compensatory and punitive damages. Champagne Demolition appears to be out of business.

ON THE ROAD
WITH TONY SABATINO

_____

July 8, 2016

Albany Business Review

Commercial real estate brokers are often on the front lines of the biggest land development and business deals, but their work happens largely behind the scenes: scoping out properties, representing clients, shuttling contracts back and forth.

Tony Sabatino at Realty USA in Colonie is consistently among the top brokers in the region, with annual sales and lease volume exceeding $10 million.

Last year, he had the second-highest number of units sold or leased through the Multiple Listing Service operated by the Commercial and Industrial Real Estate Board, a trade group in Albany.

In the 26 years since he gave up a successful nightclub and bar business, Sabatino has been the top commercial broker 20 times at Realty USA.

For these reasons, and more, I asked if I could spend several hours shadowing him on a recent day to understand how he gets the job done. I knew I would be in for some great insights. And funny stories.

He didn't disappoint.

"If you love what you do, you can make money," he told me. "I'm 67 years old, and I can't wait to get to work."

10:30 AM

Sabatino is standing in the driveway of his home on Menand Road in Loudonville wearing a monogrammed white shirt, yellow tie and tan pants. The bright sun tints his eyeglasses. It's hot.

He's on the phone, scribbling notes on a legal pad resting on the trunk of a white Toyota Avalon he leased three months ago.

He'll put upwards of 20,000 miles on the new car within a year.

Sabatino is always busy, but more so today because the day before he was co-chair of the annual Christian Brothers Academy golf outing at Albany Country Club.

He's a proud 1967 CBA grad. The outing was a "tremendous success," Sabatino said. But they took his phone away while he played. That night, he had 359 emails and 76 text messages, many of which were work-related.

"I knew I was coming back to a hell-on-Earth Tuesday," he said before checking another email.

"Oh, here we go," he said, his voice trailing off. "I got a load. I got a freakin' load. I've got [stuff] going on. I'm telling you, you couldn't have picked it any better."

He's not upset, just anxious to get going. He's been up since 6 a.m. and has already been in the office answering emails and picking up files he needs for an 11 a.m. appointment in Rensselaer.

But first, he has to get out of the driveway of the modest, red-brick home where he lives with his wife, Janis. They have two children, Emily and Philip, and three grandchildren.

Janis is also an agent at Realty USA. She sells homes, not commercial property, but she helps him stay on top of everything.

The smartphone is a double-edged sword for Sabatino. It keeps him constantly connected. But he often finds himself sitting in the car, swiping the screen as the minutes tick by.

Tony Sabatino, associate broker,
Hanna Commercial Real Estate [formerly Realty USA].
[Photo by Donna Abbott-Vlahos, courtesy of *Albany Business Review*]

The legal pad is now resting on the dashboard, within easy reach to jot down more notes.

"I've always carried a pad, always," he said. "I write things down at the end of the night. I want that. I'm 67. I'm stuck in my old-fashioned way, but you know what, don't argue with me, because it [the iPhone] works."

He hooks up the Bluetooth, and we're on our way. Next call: Joe Van De Loo. Sabatino tells him we'll be there 15 minutes later than expected.

Van De Loo owns 90 acres of undeveloped land along the Hudson River across from the Port of Albany. Sabatino just got the listing, and wants a closer look at the property.

He has a longstanding relationship with many of his clients, including Van De Loo.

"I graduated CBA with his brother, John, but I've known the family three-quarters of my life," he said. "We're all CBA graduates. Joe knows my real estate record."

11:10 AM

"I'd give anything for a couple of chocolate milks and four of those babies," Sabatino said as we approached Hot Dog Charlie's on Routes 9 and 20 in Rensselaer.

There was no time to eat as we headed toward the Port of Rensselaer. We were soon winding our way past large fuel tanks, 18-wheelers and dump trucks on the east side of the Hudson River.

The scenery then abruptly changed from industrial to pastoral.

Sabatino stopped the car next to a large cornfield. A row of trees blocked the view of the river. There's no sign to announce it, but we had quietly passed into the town of East Greenbush.

The land we were staring at is part of the 90 acres being put up for sale at $70,000 per acre, or $6.3 million total.

A car approached from the rear. I assumed it was Van De Loo, especially when the vehicle slowed and Sabatino stuck his head through the open passenger-side window to talk. A moment later, though, the driver pulled away.

Sabatino smiled broadly. The unexpected visitor was retired Albany Police Chief Bob Wolfgang, who was checking on some properties on behalf of the Port of Albany. The port, as it happens, may be interested in Van De Loo's land.

The encounter in this out-of-the-way place was sheer coincidence. Sabatino had another word for it: magical.

"I've got a hell of a life," he said. "I just love my life. Why would this happen? The one day we're here. I put my head in there and told him what we're doing. I'm not stupid. I said, 'I'm going to market this now. I can't wait, Bobby. It's all charted out.'"

We return to the car and head back the way we came because of a miscommunication about the meeting place. We find Van De Loo and he leads us down a bumpy gravel road through thick brush toward the river.

"This is like being in the Savanna," Sabatino said, continuing a running commentary of everything we see and do. "The last thing you want to get is a flat."

We finally reach the riverfront. But Sabatino doesn't get out of the car yet because another call comes in, this one from a downtown Albany building owner concerned about his listing with Sabatino. The brief conversation gets a little testy.

"Look it, I don't want to sound phony," Sabatino tells the client. "I don't care about the money. I'm trying to help you. It's time for you to get out of there ... There's no collusion going on. You're protected. Everything is kosher."

The call ends, and the tension dissipates.

Minutes later, Sabatino is snapping pictures of the riverfront on his digital camera and talking to Van De Loo about the property.

They're both encouraged by the timing of the listing and the location, given all the activity happening across the river at the port.

Van De Loo said he talked to other brokers before putting the property up for sale, but felt most comfortable with Sabatino.

"Tony's knowledge and his experience is the differentiator," Van De Loo said.

12:30 PM

Sabatino juggles 30 to 40 listings at any given time, including his next appointment: an office formerly occupied by an eye doctor. He needs to measure the space and count the number of rooms so he's prepared to answer questions from prospective tenants.

Like others who sell or lease real estate, Sabatino only gets a commission check when a deal closes.

Land mines are everywhere.

"One time we had a gentleman purchasing land," he recalled. "He went to Israel and died the week before the closing."

It wasn't the first time he had to contend with a sudden death or surprise.

In 1990, after many years owning The Lamp Post and LP's Night Club, a wildly successful college bar and dance club on Western Avenue in Albany, he wanted to do something different because he was spending so much time away from his family.

He tried selling homes.

A friend's sister moving from North Carolina to Albany wanted to buy a brownstone on Clinton Avenue. She arranged to meet Sabatino at the bar. When he reached for a pen so she could sign the purchase contract, the woman fell backwards off the bar stool, went into convulsions and died in front of him.

The next deal wasn't any better.

A couple going through a divorce got into a fight at the closing table. The wife lunged at her estranged husband with one of her high heels, striking the man in the head.

Sabatino lasted just three months. Fortunately, Realty USA was starting a new commercial division. Carol Vierath, a leader in real estate sales, called Sabatino and said he'd be a good fit because of his business background.

He sat through a training course with Vierath and two other women who became his mentors, Dottie Merza and Phyllis Barbera.

"They were three of the brightest women in commercial real estate that anybody could ever have," he said.

Still, the experience was initially frustrating.

"Commercial doesn't just happen overnight," he said. "I worked on properties that took me three years, four years to sell."

Savings, plus rental income from properties he and his wife owned near the bar in Albany, carried him through the lean years when his children were young.

"My goal was to make $50,000 [in commissions]," he said. "I'd say it took about 10 years to have a constant, good cash flow. In the last 10 years, it's been six figures."

The countless contacts he made through the nightclub helped build his real estate business.

The Sabatino name is also well-known in Albany from the days when his father, Philip, owned a liquor store on Quail Street. His dad was best friends with the city's legendary former mayor, Erastus Corning II, a Democrat who held office for 41 years.

Name recognition only goes so far, though.

"You have to perform," he said. "This is a no-nonsense business."

The keys to success are basic, he said: knowledge, honesty, serving the best interests of clients.

"You don't have to have a juris doctorate," he said. "You don't have to have a medical degree. You have to have an understanding of people. Yes, you have to know buildings, you have to know information about these buildings, you have to know city ordinances. But it's common sense."

1 PM

There's a dank, musty smell inside 288 Lark St., a building that for many years was a popular bar but is now an empty shell in search of a new owner and life.

Sabatino is walking through the place with Joe Bottillo, a sales associate at Realty USA. Bottillo needs to show Sabatino some water stains in a rear mechanical closet.

Sabatino isn't happy with what he finds on the second floor roof.

"Good God, almighty," he said while looking at a drainage pipe. "Even I can see this. Didn't the roofer come and see this? That's where the water is coming from. All right, I've got to get the roofer back."

The building is attached to the one next door at 286 Lark St. They've been on the market for about a year. The list price was dropped from $374,000 to $335,000. Thus far, potential buyers won't offer more than $300,000.

"Most of the calls I get is people who want to do a first-floor business and upper floor residential," Sabatino said.

There's no deal in sight. He's faced bigger challenges over the years.

"I've got people going through a wicked divorce that have to sell the property," he said. "I've got people that have a tax problem and they've entrusted me to get the job done. I've got people that have terminal cancer that don't have a long time to live that have said, 'Tony, you've got to get the job done.' And I've done it."

Sabatino had his own health crisis a year ago.

His typically busy life was in overdrive as he cared for his elderly father, who was living with him and Janis.

Sabatino was overweight and would get short of breath walking up a flight of stairs.

"I tried to burn the candle at both ends," he said, "and it was my greatest challenge."

One day he felt tightness in his chest. He happened to be driving by Albany Memorial Hospital, walked into the emergency room, and wound up on the operating room table.

He now has a stent in his heart, and has lost 30 pounds. His dad, who's 91 and suffers from Alzheimer's, was moved to Teresian House after he fell several times.

Sabatino wants to shed more pounds, but that doesn't stop him from suggesting a new restaurant to grab lunch: Crave, a hamburger and frozen yogurt business that opened last August inside a building he owns at the corner of Western Avenue and Quail Street.

We're sitting at a counter facing the front window, biting into juicy cheeseburgers that leave your fingers deliciously greasy.

Across the street is the building where Sabatino spent so many years running the bar and nightclub with his friend, Roger Martel. A few steps away is the liquor store his father owned for more than three decades.

"I worked at the liquor store all the time," he said. "My kids hardly knew me. I would work at the store, go to the Lamp Post, go home, take a nap, come back and stay the night. My life was working on this corner. When the toilet broke, I went and fixed it. When there was a problem with a tenant, I addressed the issue. I was busy all the time."

He doesn't miss the bar, and tries to talk people out of opening a restaurant unless they have experience. But he took a chance on Kaytrin Della Sala and Devin Ziemann, the young owners of Crave who combined their culinary and creative skills, and passion for food, to start their business.

"He took a huge risk going with Devin and I," Della Salla said. "We're very fortunate."

Lunch is done. Sabatino has to get back to the office for a 3 p.m. meeting where he'll be handed a check. It's the deposit for the former Michael's Banquet House on Route 9 in Latham, which he listed for $1.38 million.

He said he will eventually slow down, but never retire.

"Mentally, I love the rush," he said. "I love trying to out-think the impossible. My brain is rapid-fire. It's funny, until I matured, I thought everybody thought the way I did. Until I got in the ring and went, 'Oh my God, the competition is not as strong as I thought.'"

*　*　*

Tony Sabatino is still a commercial real estate broker, but now his only son, Philip, works beside him at Howard Hanna Commercial Real Estate, which merged in 2016 with Realty USA.

Philip, 36, left a marketing job in the fragrance industry to join his dad. It's fitting since Tony left behind other interests many years ago to work alongside his father.

"It's really very exciting to see him grow into this business," Tony said. "It's not an easy business. Only 5 to 10 percent of the people make six-figures. You really have to work at it. You've got to love it."

RETAILERS HIRE 'HUMAN BILLBOARDS'

February 13, 2006
Albany Business Review

Why was a 21-year-old, laid-off Christmas tree farmhand from a tiny town in northern Pennsylvania standing on a sidewalk along busy Route 7 in Latham for three days straight?

He was a walking billboard for a children's clothing store, 4 Ever Kids.

Cain Dieffenbach is one of the small legion of sign holders hired by local and national retail stores to get the word out — literally — about end-of-season discounts and going-out-of-business sales.

These aren't the people who get paid to dress in funny costumes and wave at cars.

These are the people who get paid to stand on a street corner holding a big sign with bright letters.

That's it.

For hours at a time, as if they're one picketer at a phantom rally.

If they're lucky, as Dieffenbach was during his recent stint, the winter weather is unseasonably mild. Even so, he came prepared with long johns, thermal socks, hunting gloves and a red knit hat that matched his Chuck Taylor Converse sneakers.

Asked how much he gets paid, Dieffenbach said it's about minimum wage. A friend back home owns a small company that offers the sign service, and Dieffenbach figured he could make some money now that the Christmas tree-cutting season is over.

He said the worst part was the five-hour drive from his home in Canton, Pa., to Latham because he gets carsick.

"I could stand still, but I'd rather walk around," the polite, soft-spoken Dieffenbach said as traffic roared by Peter Harris Plaza one day in January.

Although town residents sometimes complain about the practice, Colonie's sign ordinance has no prohibition against it.

"It's a free-speech issue," said Bob Cordell, chief commercial building inspector. "I can't regulate it. I can regulate signs, but I cannot regulate somebody's ability to communicate. If the sign is by itself on the ground, that's a different story."

The town of Guilderland takes a completely different stance.

Temporary signs are forbidden without a permit or zoning variance. As a result, Zoning Enforcement Officer Rodger Stone occasionally investigates calls about human billboards, particularly around Crossgates Mall. He said most retailers put a halt to the advertising once they learn about the town's laws, but not everyone agrees to stop.

Whitehall Jewelers in Crossgates is an example. The store has held a liquidation sale for the past couple of months as it prepares to close, one of 77 locations shutting down in the Chicago-based chain.

Stone said he warned Whitehall Jewelers to stop around Christmas, but the signs were back Jan. 23. He wrote an appearance ticket for violating the sign ordinance, an infraction that could result in a fine of several hundred dollars.

In six years, Stone said only two or three businesses have been fined. The charge was dropped in other cases when the violators promised not to do it anymore.

John Pytleski, manager at Whitehall Jewelers, called the ticket "absurd." He said it's not the store's problem because a liquidation company holding the going-out-of-business sale hired the sign holders.

Regardless, Pytleski said the prohibition was ridiculous.

"It's not like we're on Madison Avenue or Fifth Avenue in New York City," he said. "This is Albany."

84-YEAR-OLD DENTIST STILL KNOWS THE DRILL

December 30, 2001

The Daily Gazette

On a recent morning, Dr. Fred Isabella was at work in his small dental office in Schenectady, the last room on the left in a practice run by his son-in-law.

It's not your typical dentist office, and he's not your run-of-the-mill dentist.

The blue vinyl chair has cracks that look like earthquake fault lines, evidence of the countless number of patients who have sat, squirmed and fidgeted while Isabella had his hands, or a sharp tool, in their mouth.

On a wall behind the chair are a counter and rack displaying what could be artifacts from a Museum of Orthodontic History: stainless steel pliers, teeth trays and an electric heater for warming putty. The instruments work just as well today as they did decades ago.

Above the counter is a framed letter from Howard J. Hubbard, bishop of the Albany Roman Catholic Diocese, thanking Isabella for the 50 years he has provided free dental care to the Discalced Carmelites, a cloistered order of nuns at the Monastery of St. Teresa of Jesus in Schenectady.

"Every time I go home, my wife says, 'Fred when are you gonna quit?' " said Isabella, who looks 10 years younger than his real age, 84. "I don't want to quit."

Isabella, who became a licensed dentist in 1947, continues to work up to 16 hours a week. He shares space with his son-in-law, Dr. F. Peter Coppola, whose offices are on the first floor of a two-family house at 2325 Broadway in the Bellevue neighborhood.

Isabella stays in practice because he can. He'd work even more were it not for the health problems of his wife, Helen.

His list of patients exceeds 50, and most were with him when he had a practice with two of his brothers downtown. Both brothers have since died, and Isabella moved into his son-in-law's offices 11 years ago.

These days, he cleans teeth and makes dentures, crowns and bridges. Extractions and root canals he hands over to son-in-law Peter.

"I'll accept some new patients, but they got to be in good shape," he said in his raspy voice. "I used to pull teeth like water. Now I got too small a room."

Isabella doesn't know of another dentist in the region as old as him. He looks up at a class picture from 1970 of the Schenectady County Dental Society and said practically everyone in the photo is dead. The handful alive are no longer working, he said.

According to the American Dental Association, Isabella is in a select group. Nationally, 85 percent of dentists retire between 55 and 65 years old. In New York, 11.3 percent of dentists are still practicing over the age of 65. Still, it's not common to find a dentist working into his 80s.

"I would say it's more unusual now than a generation ago," said Dr. Robert Westcott, executive director of the 4th District Dental Society, a regional association that stretches from Schenectady to Plattsburgh. "We used to have men in their 80s and even 90s in small towns in northern New York."

Isabella's two hearing aids, curly gray hair and weathered hands are the most visible signs of his age. He is nimble on his feet, and has a memory sharper than a metal pick. He peppers his conversation with Italian phrases, and his salty tongue would make a sailor blush. Around female patients, though, he's a gentleman.

"We like him," said Mary Prater of Schenectady, who was reclined in the chair on a recent visit. "He's a great guy."

Prater became convinced Isabella was the right dentist for her family in 1956, when he began treating her son, Lewis, at Pleasant Valley elementary school. Lewis, who is mentally handicapped, was frightened of dentists. But he was comfortable around Isabella. To this day Prater, her husband and Lewis continue seeing him.

"We like his attitude," she said.

Born in Mechanicville on Aug. 3, 1917, Isabella was one of nine children. His parents, Nicholas and Rose, emigrated from Alvignano, a small town in the Italian province of Caserta.

His father worked in a paper mill and tannery in Mechanicville before moving to Schenectady to work at the United Baking Co. bread assembly line. His mother was a seamstress.

After graduating from Mont Pleasant High School in 1936, Isabella chose to work instead of attending college like his older brother, Ralph. But his parents insisted on higher education, and he eventually enrolled in the Albany College of Pharmacy.

He graduated in 1942, but his plans for studying dentistry at the University at Buffalo got delayed because he was drafted into the Army during World War II.

He finished basic training in Florida and was supposed to go to a military camp in California, the last stop before getting shipped overseas. As luck would have it, he was accepted into an Army specialist-training program at Yale Medical School a week before he was scheduled to leave.

"I was ecstatic," he recalled.

After a few more twists and turns he accidentally reported for duty at Yale a week late. He got married in 1944 and graduated from the University at Buffalo in 1947.

Isabella joined his brother, Ennio, who already had a dental practice at 607 Union St. [Today it's the Manhattan Exchange restaurant]. Another brother, Hugo, an orthodontist, also teamed up with them.

In those days, an X-ray cost $6 and cleanings were $5.

"Guess what I made my first year?" said Isabella, who marvels at how much dentists now charge. "Three thousand bucks."

Isabella, a Democrat, was known for more than just filling cavities.

Beginning in 1958, he served on the City Council for 16 years. He then served two years in the state Senate, but the party wouldn't endorse him for re-election. He forced a primary and said he lost by 300 votes, a defeat that still burns him. Two years later, he took on state Sen. Hugh T. Farley, a Republican, but lost again.

That was his last stab at politics, but others in the family caught the bug.

His nephew, Tom Isabella, had a 16-year tenure on the City Council. His daughter, Sharon Coppola, one of five children, has served on the city Planning Commission since 1984. Sharon Coppola has never run for elected office, but would consider it down the road.

Trolling the neighborhoods for votes and making speeches at City Hall are long behind Isabella. He seems to thoroughly enjoy the time he has with his patients.

"All right, am I hurting you?" he asked Prater, who was in the chair to have work done on her caps. "No way," he said to himself.

The loud wee of a drill filled the air.

"Turn that way," he said, pausing. "At-a-girl."

She complied, and he gently pinched her nose.

*   *   *

Dr. Fred Isabella died November 28, 2007. He was 90.

"Rooms lit up when Dr. Freddy entered, and he made everyone feel important," his cousins, Fred and Betty Miranda and Marilyn Miranda-Bocchi of Saratoga Springs, wrote in the online guest book. "His sense of humor was enjoyed by his patients and family."

Isabella was a customer of John Grady's one-hour photo business. Isabella would stay and chat when he was dropping off film.

"I will miss him," Grady wrote.

A HOME IN
SCHENECTADY

GUYANESE MIGRATION INTO CITY PICKS UP STEAM

April 6, 2003

The Daily Gazette

On a breezy, mild Friday night, when much of the Capital Region was swept up in the NCAA basketball tournament or the somber news of war in Iraq, a U-Haul truck lumbered down McClellan Street toward a darkened two-family house.

The driver, Devaram Malchan, pulled up to 410-412 McClellan, stepped out of the truck and glanced up at the vinyl-sided yellow house. The three-bedroom, first-floor flat will be the new home for him, his wife and their three daughters.

At $500 a month, the rent is about half what the Malchans paid for a one-bedroom apartment in Jamaica, Queens. The savings, he said, was worth the risk of leaving his job stocking merchandise at Macy's with no guarantee he would be transferred to a similar position locally.

He hopes it will take less than a year to join the growing ranks of Guyanese who have become homeowners, something that would have been impossible on his salary in New York City.

"That's my aim," Malchan, 42, said as a handful of friends and relatives helped him unload couches, stereo speakers and mattresses from the truck.

In the past few years, the migration of Guyanese and other West Indians to Schenectady has happened at such a fast clip there is no reliable count on how many have moved here. Based on estimates provided by local officials, clergy and businessmen, about 3,000 have settled in the city.

Like Malchan, most are drawn by the prospect of living in a quieter, slower-paced environment where home ownership is within reach. Houses that sell for $60,000 or less in Schenectady would cost $270,000 or more in parts of Queens and Brooklyn.

Although they have been welcomed with open arms by Mayor Albert P. Jurczynski and other residents, there have also been rumblings of discontent and suspicions about their motives. In that way, they are no different from Italians, Poles, French, Germans, blacks and other ethnic or racial groups that have settled in Schenectady throughout the city's 205-year history.

The Guyanese, as it happens, have been on the move for decades. Since the late 1960s, tens of thousands have left the poor South American nation of Guyana for the United States and Canada, most settling in New York City and Toronto.

Many were Indo-Guyanese rice farmers and sugar workers who trace their roots to the days when the country was a British colony and indentured servants were brought from India to work in the fields. Others are Afro-Guyanese — descendants of slaves who worked on plantations.

Scores of middle class professionals also left to seek a better life.

English is their official language, though many speak with a Caribbean-flavored dialect that can be hard to understand.

There has been a tiny population of Guyanese in Schenectady County for at least 15 years. According to the 2000 Census, 360 people identified themselves as being of Guyanese descent, with the heaviest concentration in the city.

Their numbers have grown exponentially in the past few years, as evidenced by the conversion of a closed Catholic church in Mont Pleasant to a vibrant Hindu temple, and the swelling congregations at Christ Family Fellowship and Spirit & Truth Christian Church.

Most Guyanese are Christian or Hindu. There has also been a migration of people who are natives of other West Indian countries, such as Trinidad and Tobago.

The steady movement from New York City was already under-way when Jurczynski first learned about the changes taking place in the city where he was born and raised.

Jurczynski, the grandson of Polish and French-Canadian immigrants, began to identify with the newcomers and admire what he saw as a desire to work hard, invest in their homes and help each other.

"They made it very clear that unless it's absolutely necessary, they don't believe in people going on welfare," Jurczynski recalled of his first meeting with a group of Guyanese about two years ago at the new Schenectady Hindu Temple in Mont Pleasant.

"That's the way I was brought up," he continued. "I'm not against people having public assistance that deserve to be, like people with disabilities. But my grandparents that came from Poland always were very proud of the fact they came to this country with nothing and they never collected a day's worth of public assistance in their life."

Over the past year, the mayor has dived headfirst into an effort he considers Schenectady's best chance to recover from decades of financial decline and population exodus: convincing even more Guyanese and other West Indians to move north, buy houses, find jobs and open small businesses.

So far, it seems to be working, although the changes have been more gradual than sweeping. Schenectady today still looks very much like the depressed, struggling city it was in the late 1990s.

Yet, one- and two-family houses are selling faster and at higher prices than they have in six years. Tax-foreclosed properties that the city could barely give away a few years ago in Hamilton Hill and other neighborhoods are now fetching multiple offers. A handful of small grocery stores has opened.

Walter Chintomby said he recently sold his house in the Flushing neighborhood of Queens for $650,000. With that money he bought a one-family house on Chrisler Avenue for him and his wife; a two-family in Hamilton Hill he plans to give to one of his grown sons; and the E-Z Cue at 1410 State St.

He plans to convert what was a rowdy pool hall into a top-notch restaurant and bring in Guyanese pop star Terry Gajraj for the grand opening this summer.

"When I first came up here [to visit] there was hardly any Guyanese," said Chintomby, a real estate agent who traveled frequently to Schenectady over the past 15 years visiting relatives and friends. "Now, everywhere you go, you see them. If you go to Home Depot, that's the place to go."

A Guyanese family moved in across from Martha Pentinen on Front Street in the Stockade about a year ago. She's very pleased with the improvements they did to their property.

"I can't say enough good things about the Guyanese people I have had contact with," said Pentinen, 80, a lifelong city resident and retired GE worker who also ran the elevator at the old Carl Co. store downtown.

While some residents have hailed the new investment and cultural diversity, others are expressing resentment and skepticism toward the Guyanese and the mayor for what he's doing.

Councilman Joseph Allen, the only black elected official in the city, has said he welcomes the new Guyanese homeowners, but has criticized Jurczynski for singling them out as hard-working people.

Allen has pointed out that many blacks — including his late father, who held down a second job at a candy store — worked in the factories that made Schenectady an industrial powerhouse during the first half of the 20th century.

Contrary to what the mayor has said about the Guyanese avoiding welfare, there have been whispers some are receiving public assistance. No data is available because the Schenectady County Department of Social Services doesn't keep track of an applicant's nationality.

"I would say, just generally, if you had someone working and they didn't have medical insurance, they'd be free to apply for Medicaid, Child Health Plus or Family Health Plus," Social Services Commissioner Dennis J. Packard said. "As to whether they were financially eligible, that would be determined on a case-by-case basis."

As properties change hands, some city residents who live in multi-unit buildings have been displaced or complained about their new landlords.

Christina Sferra was living in a small one-bedroom unit on the second floor of the E-Z Cue when Chintomby bought the pool hall in January.

Sferra described herself as being "in recovery" and behind on her $275 monthly rent. Chintomby evicted her, and several others for lack of payment. He said he is being more selective than the previous owner about who can live upstairs.

A tenant who lives in another building has had problems with her Guyanese landlords, but doesn't believe complaining to the mayor will do any good because he has been "rolling out the red carpet" for the newcomers. She didn't want her name printed in the newspaper because she feared she could be evicted.

A myth that has been circulating in Schenectady is that the Guyanese newcomers don't have to pay property taxes for seven years. Ed Waterfield, supervisor of the tax-receipts bureau, could only laugh and shake his head in disbelief when he heard that one. No, he said, it's not true.

There's no question the new residents have had to contend with the realities of finding and keeping jobs, and of becoming homeowners in Schenectady.

One company that employs about 150 Guyanese, Contec Corp., recently laid off about 24 people because of a slowdown in the repair of cable TV set-top boxes. A company official said the layoffs were only a seasonal adjustment, and the workers may be brought back. About 525 people, including administrative staff, work there.

At City Hall, in the Bureau of Tax Receipts, new Guyanese homeowners have shown up almost daily asking questions since tax bills were mailed in late December.

Some are shocked to learn how much they owe. Others didn't realize they also have to pay a separate school tax bill.

JURCZYNSKI PLAYING BIG ROLE
IN INFLUX OF GUYANESE

April 6, 2003

The Daily Gazette

"Hello Mr. Mayor," came the greeting from a man sipping a drink as Albert P. Jurczynski stepped inside the Kaieteur Restaurant & Sports Bar to have lunch with a couple of local businessmen on a recent afternoon.

Jurczynski needs few introductions when he stops by the Kaieteur or many of the other businesses that line the bustling avenues of Richmond Hill, Queens, the hub of Guyanese life in New York City.

The mayor has made the 175-mile trip from Schenectady in his city-owned Chevy Lumina so many times over the past year that he has little trouble navigating the clogged expressways and bridges to reach the heart of the neighborhood.

He has become a celebrity of sorts — the white Republican politician from the small upstate city who greets everyone with a wide smile and beefy handshake; who encourages small-business owners to open a second store in Schenectady; who has developed a taste for spicy West Indian cuisine and a splash of El Dorado rum.

Three Sundays ago, he got on stage at a neighborhood park in Richmond Hill and spoke to tens of thousands of people celebrating the Hindu festival of Pagwah, a rite of spring best known for dowsing one another with brightly colored powders.

More recently, he attended another Pagwah celebration, this one at a Hindu temple in Schenectady.

Jurczynski, a Catholic whose ancestry is Polish and French Canadian and whose wife is Italian, clearly enjoys the cross-cultural experiences.

On Wednesday, he leaves for a weeklong trip to Guyana, a poor, English-speaking country on the northeast coast of South America, to learn even more about Schenectady's newest inhabitants.

His enthusiasm has resonated with the Guyanese and people from the West Indies. That welcoming attitude has been an important factor in helping to encourage a migration of Guyanese upstate in search of more affordable housing and a slower pace of life.

Many have bought what were run-down properties on the city's most distressed streets and renovated them into tidy homes. Some have decorative white, wrought-iron fences in front, a reminder of the style popular in their native Guyana.

They have found jobs at local hospitals, nursing homes, schools and various private companies. Others have opened their own businesses.

But, for all the improvements in the real estate market, and glowing stories about Jurczynski's efforts in the national and international media, there has been a mixed reaction at home.

Some residents are upset because they believe Jurczynski is showing preferential treatment to the Guyanese in housing and job fairs. They also doubt there's enough employment to sustain the newcomers.

They get suspicious when they see boarded-up houses get purchased in Hamilton Hill but remain vacant eyesores. And, they think Jurczynski is just trying to recruit new Republican voters in a city dominated by Democrats.

"I'm trying to be fair, but I haven't heard anything good," said a 74-year-old man from the upper Union Street neighborhood who didn't want to be identified. "It's better to stay away from them."

Former Schenectady Mayor Al Jurczynski
at a grocery store in Richmond Hills, Queens [Photo by Michael DeMasi]

One woman wrote a letter to the editor that in effect told the Guyanese: Stop coming here.

Others have been less direct, but still critical.

Jurczynski believes the majority of residents support his efforts, and that the backlash has come from a small group of people or political opponents.

"I have been a little surprised at some people that have not embraced this," Jurczynski said. "They're very careful in what they say, but I can sense that they're not happy. I'm not going to get into names. They're not elected officials. It's people I've known for a long, long time.

"The funny thing is, they're ethnics themselves," he continued. "You would think they would understand because one of the things I sensed in my lifetime is the things that have been said about me being Polish. It's based in ignorance and in bigotry."

If the recruitment effort has helped Jurczynski politically — or the Republican Party in the city as a whole — the gains are not readily apparent.

Membership in the Republican Party in Schenectady fell by about 575 voters between 2001 and 2002. Democratic enrollments also decreased, but the party continues to maintain a big advantage over Republicans, 12,782 to 8,834, according to the Schenectady County Board of Elections.

Some of the Guyanese and West Indians who have moved here aren't U.S. citizens, let alone registered voters.

While the local impact on Jurczynski's political fortunes is hard to gauge, he has certainly made an impression with Republicans at the state level.

Through his contacts, the mayor helped organize a fund-raiser for Gov. George E. Pataki in Richmond Hill last fall that generated $50,000 for the governor's re-election campaign.

The event was particularly noteworthy because business leaders there are accustomed to supporting Democrats in statewide and national races.

"The governor is reaching out to all minority groups," said Kawal Totaram, an attorney and influential Democrat in Richmond Hill. "While at first brush it would [seem] the mayor was instrumental, I think the governor wants to stretch his hand beyond the traditional Republican groups."

Whether Jurczynski will mount another campaign after 20 years in elected office as a councilman and mayor is a question that has been dogging him for months.

Most expected last month he would announce he wasn't going to run for a third, four-year term, but he put off the decision until after he returns from Guyana on April 15.

Democrats are practically licking their chops over the prospect of running against an administration that has been tainted in the past few years by a police corruption scandal; a fiscal crisis that caused the city's credit rating to plummet to junk-bond status; and a disastrous snow plowing effort after a nearly 2-foot storm last Christmas.

Democratic county Legislator Brian U. Stratton, who has announced he's running for mayor, said Jurczynski's Guyanese initiative has been "admirable" and he welcomes the newcomers.

Still, he said, "I think his priorities perhaps are not where they should be. I think that recruitment of new families and hard-working people to Schenectady is an important thing, but there are tremendous shortcomings in this administration."

Jurczynski insists he hasn't made up his mind about whether to run, and that the desire to continue courting the Guyanese to Schenectady is the biggest factor in deciding whether to take on Stratton this fall.

"The Guyanese initiative could continue without me as mayor, [but] the question remains, will it continue at the rapid pace? I think Schenectady needs this influx to continue at the rapid pace because timing is everything, and Schenectady can't really afford to wallow."

QUEENS MAN HELPS MAYOR
ATTRACT NEW RESIDENTS

April 8, 2003
The Daily Gazette

His given name is Hemant Bhup Singh, but like other immigrants adjusting to life in America, he became known by a name easier to pronounce: Herman.

That was in 1980, at age 15, when Singh moved with his family from a rural town in the poor South American nation of Guyana to Brooklyn. A couple of years later, the Singhs settled in a section of Queens called Richmond Hill.

The area was depressed, and the housing cheaper there.

"When we were moving in, most were moving out," Singh recalled of the once-largely Italian neighborhood that has been transformed into the bustling hub of Guyanese life in New York City. "They probably went to Long Island and different parts."

Today, Singh is witnessing another great migration, this time from Richmond Hill and other areas of New York City to Schenectady. He has become one of the central figures in spreading the word about what he and others see as a golden opportunity.

Singh, 38, is sole owner of Home Link Realty and of Tropical Funding, a one-stop shop in Richmond Hill for people buying or selling real estate and shopping for a mortgage.

He is by no means the only person who has benefited from the surge of interest in buying homes in Schenectady over the past two years, but he's without question the most high profile and active among his counterparts in Queens.

That's because of the role he played in the early stages of what has become an aggressive campaign by Mayor Albert P. Jurczynski to sell Schenectady as a more affordable, safer and quieter alternative to New York City.

A tall, broad-shouldered man with wavy black hair and deep brown eyes, Singh has become very successful since leaving the accounting department of a steel factory in 1986 and going into real estate.

Home Link Realty is in a squat, one-story white stucco building that was once a bakery on busy Atlantic Avenue in Richmond Hill. Thirteen full-time and 20 part-time employees work for him. Attached to the building is a banquet hall he runs that can seat hundreds of people for weddings and other events.

Singh's office is sparsely decorated. A bookshelf lined with multi-armed statues serves as an altar to Hindu gods. One wall is full of awards bestowed on him by local community groups and politicians in Queens.

One plaque proclaims him "The King of the Airwaves" in recognition of his weekly Saturday morning radio show on WRTN 93.5 FM that blends Indian music, in-studio guests and plugs for his real estate business.

"When I first started, it wasn't easy," he said of hosting a three-hour show.

Singh wears finely tailored suits and drives a gas-devouring, maroon H2 Hummer. His other car is a white stretch Lincoln Navigator limousine, which turned plenty of heads last summer as it maneuvered through the streets of Schenectady.

Yet, for all the apparent showiness, Singh is down-to-earth.

He speaks softly. He looks people squarely in the eye and makes them feel welcome. Acquaintances say he gives freely of his time and money to help community causes and the less fortunate.

He seems proud of his heritage as a descendant of indentured servants brought to Guyana from India. As the youngest son, he carries on the cultural tradition of caring for his mother and father.

They live with him, his wife, Sindy, and their 6-year-old son, Armant, in an upscale part of Queens called Jamaica Estates.

Over the past several years, Singh had heard bits and pieces from friends and business associates about a growing Guyanese population in Schenectady.

Housing prices are dirt cheap compared to Richmond Hill, where a 1,600-square-foot single-family house on a postage stamp-sized lot can sell for $350,000.

About a year ago, Singh and a small group of businessmen arranged to meet Jurczynski in City Hall.

It was Singh's first visit to Schenectady. He wasn't impressed when he got off Interstate 890.

"I thought it was very depressed and that I didn't want to be part of this," he said.

On a later visit, he got another perspective as Jurczynski showed him and others Central Park and residential neighborhoods where the housing stock was in better shape.

Singh remembers being impressed to learn the city has two hospitals.

Jurczynski, in turn, was impressed by what he saw in Richmond Hill. The area reminded him of the Mont Pleasant neighborhood in Schenectady, except with a bustling central business district and a high percentage of owner-occupied houses.

Shortly after that, Jurczynski went on Singh's radio show to talk about the affordable houses in Schenectady. The mayor took the risky step of giving out his cellphone number on the air.

"I think they were amused more than anything," Jurczynski said. "'Geez, this guy is crazy.' When we went to commercial, Herman said to me, 'Man, are you nuts?' The phone started ringing off the hook."

Singh then began chartering buses to bring interested people on weekly trips to Schenectady.

Jurczynski and other officials greeted them at City Hall, told them about housing and job opportunities and took them on a guided tour of the city.

The visitors were amazed to have so much attention lavished on them, and to see large, single-family houses on tree-lined streets with detached garages that cost $130,000, about a quarter of the going rate in their communities.

"Our people . . . they see a white man come to our community to recruit us, for us it's good," Singh said. "That's the way we feel . . . because it was never done that way for us."

The tours really took off after the effort was profiled in *The New York Times* last July.

Singh said the story was also carried in Guyanese and Caribbean newspapers. He even got a call from a man in Trinidad interested in what was happening.

Singh estimates his office has handled at least four property closings per week as a mortgage broker or real estate agent since August, none of which were houses that were owned by the city as a result of a tax foreclosure.

The bus tours stopped over the winter, but Singh said the enthusiasm didn't wane.

He doesn't get the sense people are deterred by some of the bad news coming out of Schenectady over the past several months, including a 25 percent property tax increase and city streets crippled by a big Christmas Day snowstorm.

"The tax problem we have here, too," he said. "We have our fair share of income taxes."

Singh plans to offer the bus tours again late this month. In the meantime, he and his wife are looking to buy a home in Schenectady so they have a place to stay while here on business.

They'd like something in the GE Realty Plot, a neighborhood of stately old homes that are the priciest in the city.

*   *   *

The Guyanese migration continued in Schenectady after Mayor Al Jurczynski left office, but it was less visible without him serving as the Pied Piper.

Similar to other ethnic and racial groups that have settled in the city during its long history, some of the new residents became active in government as their numbers and influence grew.

John Mootooveren, an accountant who had formed the Guyanese American Association in Schenectady, was elected to the city council in 2013. He received more votes than any candidate on the ballot that year and was re-elected in 2017.

Two Guyanese-Americans were sworn into the police department in January 2018, a first for the city.

In early September 2018, the annual Guyana Day celebration was held in Grout Park, with food, music, games, dancing and a cricket tournament.

Suraj Jagdeo, Udesh Ramdiall and Michael Lalloo [left to right] of the Knight Riders cricket team at the annual Guyana Day celebration in Schenectady.
[Photo by Michael DeMasi]

I spoke to Jurczynski a few days after the event and he told me the Guyanese initiative was "hands down my proudest accomplishment."

While there's no doubt the Guyanese population has grown in the city, the estimate given to me by officials in 2003 — roughly 3,000 — was a little off the mark.

According to the U.S. Census Bureau's 2006-2010 American Community Survey, there were 1,999 Guyanese in Schenectady County [the margin of error was +/- 514]. The majority was presumably in the city, though the survey doesn't break the number down by municipalities in the county.

The 2011-2015 American Community Survey found 3,578 Guyanese in the county, with a margin of error of +/- 691.

I'm curious to see the total when the 2020 Census is done.

Despite the strides they have made in Schenectady, and the pride Guyanese have in the community, no ethnic group is immune from internal rivalries and clashes.

For instance, a spat with a fellow Guyanese thrust Mootooveren into the headlines in early 2018. The police charged him with harassment, a violation, after he allegedly threw an alcoholic drink in another man's face late at night inside a bar, according to The Daily Gazette. He denied the accusation and resolved the charge in city court.

LAWS
AND
ORDER

DEAD PRISONER'S WIDOW
SEARCHES FOR ANSWERS

January 12, 1997

The Post-Star

Frederick L. Matthews was in the 20th year of a 25-year-to-life prison term for murder when he was found dead of a drug overdose in his cell at Great Meadow Correctional Facility in upstate New York.

Four days later, on July 30, 1994, a funeral service was held in his hometown in New York City.

Matthews was then cremated, and his ashes remain with his widow, Deborah, an advertising editor living in the suburbs of Philadelphia.

During those few days, between the time Deborah heard a message on her answering machine from the prison chaplain to the time she attended services at Foster Phillips Funeral Home in Jamaica, Queens, something was done to Frederick's body that haunts Deborah to this day.

According to a Long Island forensic pathologist Deborah hired to perform an autopsy on her dead husband, Frederick's body was missing its brain and two other organs when it arrived for examination. The body was returned to Frederick's family in that condition for his funeral.

The organs had been removed during an earlier, state-ordered autopsy at Glens Falls Hospital.

Deborah knew about the first autopsy. She just didn't know that some of her husband's organs would be removed and never returned. To someone unfamiliar with the world of pathology and coroners, the news came as a shock.

What bothered Deborah even more is that she would have never known Frederick's brain was missing had she not paid for her own autopsy, which verified the state's cause of death.

"I think it's unconscionable that a person is taken to a hospital, an autopsy is performed, organs are removed and the family isn't notified," said Deborah, 41. "If I didn't have an autopsy done, I wouldn't have known what they had done to his body."

Health laws in New York state permit pathologists to remove and retain the brain or portions of other organs for legitimate reasons, such as determining the cause of death in a coroner's case.

But coroners, who often order autopsies, aren't required by law to disclose that information to the next of kin.

Nor does the New York State Association of County Coroners and Medical Examiners have guidelines mandating such disclosure, despite the thousands of autopsies done in the state every year.

Into this regulatory vacuum fell Deborah, who said she couldn't get an explanation from a Washington County coroner or hospital officials about what happened to Frederick's brain.

In addition to his brain, Frederick's stomach and adrenal glands were also missing, according to the report of the second autopsy, performed by Dr. Mark L. Taff of Lynbrook in Nassau County.

The first autopsy of Frederick Matthews, 41, was performed by Dr. Woong M. Lee at Glens Falls Hospital on July 27, 1994, according to an autopsy report Deborah furnished to *The Post-Star*.

The report indicates Frederick's brain was placed in a solution to harden it so that sections could be viewed under a microscope.

Lee's method of examining the brain is standard procedure in a coroner's case, according to hospital spokesman Timothy P. Riley.

Although practices vary depending on circumstances surrounding the death, placing the brain in a hardening solution — a process that takes about 10 days to two weeks — is necessary because the soft tissue could otherwise fall apart during a dissection, making it difficult to pinpoint any abnormalities, according to several pathologists in this region and elsewhere in the country.

The pathologists said small sections of other organs, measuring perhaps a few millimeters thick, are generally kept for examination, and the remainder of the organ is placed in a plastic bag inside the cadaver, which is then returned to the family for burial or cremation.

Families who request an autopsy at Glens Falls Hospital must sign a form that includes a statement that organs might be retained for further study, Riley said.

When someone dies suddenly in the hospital, a physician will sometimes suggest an autopsy to determine the cause of death. If the family consents, the autopsy is performed, although the family can set certain restrictions, such as forbidding an examination of the brain.

Those situations differ from a coroner's case, in which there is a violent or suspicious death, and the coroner is legally responsible for determining the physiological cause [such as cancer, gunshot wound or cardiopulmonary arrest] and manner of death [such as accident, suicide or homicide].

Unless a reasonable conclusion about the cause of death can be reached without an autopsy, the coroner will generally order one.

If a family objects on religious or other grounds, and there's no suspicion of foul play, a coroner might not order an autopsy, provided the cause of death is readily apparent, said Dr. Andrew W. Garner, a Warren County coroner.

Under the state's County Law, however, an autopsy must be performed on all prison inmates who die while incarcerated.

The intention behind state health laws governing autopsies is that a body be treated in a respectful manner, said Kristine A. Smith, spokeswoman of the state Health Department. If an organ is retained for a legitimate reason, such as determining the cause of death, it can later be cremated.

"I would think the vast majority of people wouldn't think about it, nor would it be a real problem for them to know that the organ has been disposed of with respect after all of the research" into the cause of death, Smith said.

Depending upon a person's religion, though, it could be a problem.

Jews, for instance, believe the body houses the soul, and the entire body should be buried after death unless a family or the deceased had agreed to donate an organ to save someone's life.

Jews object to autopsies, but realize they might not have a choice if it's required by a coroner to determine the cause of death, said Rabbi Richard J. Sobel of Temple Beth-El in Glens Falls.

Sobel didn't realize that the brain is sometimes kept after a coroner's autopsy, and believes that should be disclosed to the family.

Muslims also object to autopsies and would be upset to learn a body has been returned from a pathologist without all of its organs, said Muhammad Ahmed, an imam who works in the local prison system.

Another religious leader, the Rev. Martin J. Fisher at St. Mary's Church in Glens Falls, believes that, as a matter of ethics, a family should be told if a body might be returned from an autopsy without all of its organs.

But yet another local Catholic priest, the Rev. Thomas M. Powers, questioned the purpose of volunteering information "that would only be emotionally stressful" to a family that is already grieving.

"To what purpose?" he said.

Provided the organs are treated and disposed of in a respectful way, the church's tenets wouldn't be violated if the body is buried without all of its organs, said Powers, who teaches at St. Bernard Institute, a graduate school of theology in Albany.

The autopsy of Frederick Matthews was one of many performed at Glens Falls Hospital and across the state in 1994 at the direction of a coroner. That year, there were 96 coroner autopsies at Glens Falls Hospital, Riley said.

According to the state Health Department, 1,682 coroner autopsies were performed that year in New York.

Other autopsies in the state were performed under the direction of a medical examiner, coroner's physician or other health official. The total number of autopsies in 1994 was 19,226.

Coroners are elected officials in New York state and need not be physicians. Those who aren't physicians must appoint one to perform autopsies. The system varies by region, and some areas, such as New York City, have medical examiners who must be physicians.

The issue of whether coroners should disclose detailed information to a family prior to an autopsy hasn't been raised locally, according to several coroners.

Nor has it arisen among members of the state Association of County Coroners and Medical Examiners, which has about 170 paid members, said William J. Stahl of Putnam County, who serves on the group's board of directors.

"That's something I haven't even thought about," Stahl said when asked whether there's a need for uniform policy among coroners in the state.

Stahl, who serves as chief coroner in Putnam County, said he would tell a family after an autopsy is completed whether an organ was retained for testing.

In his 18 years as a coroner, that has happened only once, Stahl said, when a young boy was killed after his liver ruptured in a school bus accident. In all the autopsies he has witnessed, Stahl added, the entire brain was never kept by the pathologist.

Several local coroners question the wisdom of burdening a grieving family with the gruesome details of an autopsy.

"I think it's traumatic enough to tell them it [the autopsy] has to be done," said Dr. Leonard Busman, a retired general practitioner who has served as a Warren County coroner for more than 10 years.

Dr. B. Peter Jensen, a Washington County coroner for about 11 years, believes most people are aware that organs or blood or tissue samples might be retained for the purpose of determining the cause of death. He said he doesn't see the value in informing those who might not understand the procedure.

"You don't load people down at that time with technical discussions," Jensen said.

Another Washington County coroner, Donald R. Pushee, said he would inform a family that inquired about details of the autopsy. But he said he wouldn't otherwise volunteer information about autopsy procedures.

"I think you're just stirring up trouble," Pushee said of any sort of disclosure requirement.

Yet Deborah Matthews said she would have preferred to know the facts before Frederick's funeral and cremation.

"As difficult as it would have been to have been told, I would have preferred to be told up front than to find out the way I did, with all the suspicion surrounding it," said Deborah, who still does not know what became of the organs and whether they were used for medical research or some other unauthorized purpose.

To this day, despite a phone conversation with Washington County Coroner Edward F. Parsons and letters written by her and her attorneys to Glens Falls Hospital, Deborah said she still hasn't been told what became of Frederick's brain and other organs.

Generally speaking, organ tissues that are removed from the body are eventually disposed of as medical waste, which means they are cremated, said Riley, the hospital's spokesman. But Riley wouldn't comment on the specifics of the autopsy on Frederick Matthews.

Riley said the county coroner who handled the case, Parsons, must be contacted for that information. Although the autopsy was done at the hospital, the coroner has legal authority over the reports.

Parsons refused to discuss the Matthews autopsy with *The Post-Star* because, he said, there is a civil suit pending and the information is confidential between him and the family. Deborah has filed an unrelated civil suit in another county over Frederick's treatment while he was incarcerated.

Deborah said she called Parsons in December 1994 to ask about the missing brain, stomach and adrenal glands. She said she was told they were not sent to the State Police crime lab for toxicology tests. Parsons "really backed off" when she asked what became of the brain, adding he didn't know anything about it, she said.

In a routine autopsy, if the brain is hardened and examined, a portion is kept in a stock bottle for a couple of years in case further questions arise about the medical condition of the deceased, and the remainder is cremated, said Dr. Marcella F. Fierro, chief medical examiner for the state of Virginia and chairman of the forensic pathologist committee of the College of American Pathologists.

The brain tissue in the stock bottle is also eventually cremated, said Fierro, who added there is no law in Virginia requiring the family be contacted and asked if they prefer to have the organ buried with the body. Nor has it been the practice of pathologists in that state to contact families, Fierro said.

"I'm not sure families would be pleased to get a phone call three years after the fact saying we have pieces of your brother's brain," Fierro said.

In New York, once tests are completed, families should get to decide whether they want to have organs disposed of by the hospital or interred with the body, said Smith, the state Health Department's spokeswoman.

"That usually doesn't happen, frankly, because in most cases people don't want to go through another burial. They want some closure," Smith said.

Deborah didn't know Frederick in 1974 when he began serving a prison term for killing a man in Queens. It wasn't until 1987 that Deborah met him through a mutual friend while he was serving time at the state prison in Attica.

Frederick became godfather to one of their mutual friend's children, and Deborah was asked to be godmother. Deborah, who was single, fell in love with Frederick.

"I found a very intelligent and articulate and communicative man," Deborah said, "which certainly broke any stereotype I had in mind of someone incarcerated."

Photocopies provided by Deborah show Frederick earned an associate's degree from Genesee Community College in 1977 and a bachelor's from Canisius College of Buffalo in 1979 while in prison.

Frederick was eventually moved to Green Haven Correctional Facility in Dutchess County. He and Deborah married in 1991. Later, Frederick was transferred to Clinton Correctional Facility in Dannemora and, in 1994, to Great Meadow.

Throughout his incarceration, Frederick had disciplinary problems and suffered two documented cases of drug overdose in 1993, according to the state Commission of Correction's final report on his death.

Deborah said she didn't know of Frederick's drug use.

"It hurts me to think he had a drug problem and I wasn't aware of it," Deborah said. "If this was the problem he had, then I can't judge him because I did not walk in his shoes and I would not want to walk in his shoes that long [in prison]. Prison shouldn't be a Holiday Inn, but there are certain dignities that should be afforded every human being."

After learning of Frederick's death, an attorney at Prisoners' Legal Services in Plattsburgh advised Deborah to pay for her own autopsy.

"The attorney said get the body out of there as soon as possible," Deborah recalled. "And get a private autopsy performed. Not to believe the state's autopsy."

Deborah said she later received some information from a lawyer who said Frederick might have been intentionally given a lethal dose of cocaine and heroin in retaliation for supposedly tipping off a corrections officer about a drug shipment coming to the prison.

However, neither the State Police nor state Commission of Correction turned up any evidence of foul play.

* * *

I wasn't able to track down Deborah Matthews to see if she ever learned from medical officials what happened to her husband's brain and other organs after he died.

GASTON HOOKS JR. ISN'T A COP, BUT HE DRESSES LIKE ONE

June 15, 2003
The Daily Gazette

Gaston Hooks Jr. isn't a police officer, a sheriff's deputy or even a bailiff who watches over courtrooms, but that's where the line between reality and perception often gets blurry.

Hooks is a self-appointed sergeant and investigator at his own legal services company, Court Process Division, at 1001 State St. in Schenectady.

He has the uniform to prove it.

His black shirt and matching Dickies pants, wide-brimmed hat, two walkie-talkies, whistle and handcuffs all look like standard-issue police gear.

There's a U.S. flag patch stitched to his right sleeve, an eagle on the left sleeve, and gold sergeant stripes on both. Clipped to his shirt collar are the initials "C.P.D."

Even the three black-and-white cars he drives look official, emblazoned with the word "Eviction" and stars that are labeled Court Process Division. The station wagon is billed as the "K-9 Unit."

All of this has made Hooks a very well-known — and in some quarters, distrusted — person in the world of evictions, a place where landlords and tenants tussle on a daily basis over late rents, shoddy apartments and disputes over who's-scamming-who.

Landlords, many of which live outside Schenectady, routinely hire Hooks to serve legal notice on tenants who are being evicted. He also serves as a property manager at many apartments — a dual role that some officials say creates further confusion for tenants.

He has become a fixture on the second floor of City Hall, appearing before City Court Judge Guido A. Loyola during eviction hearings or standing in the hallway waiting for his turn to be called, his heavy-set frame decked out in a uniform.

Hooks insists he provides a valuable service to landlords who don't want to confront tenants on their own, and that his outfit sends a message he won't be pushed around when serving eviction notices. The paperwork he hands out clearly states he's not a law enforcement officer.

"Just because somebody is doing something different from other people, doesn't make it wrong," the soft-spoken Hooks, 47, said during a recent interview outside the courtroom.

Yet, Hooks' uniform and demeanor with tenants are troubling to advocates who work on behalf of people facing eviction.

They say tenants who aren't aware of their rights are led to believe Hooks is a sheriff's deputy, and he creates the impression they have three days to get out. Some have moved immediately.

"It's just deceiving," said Jane Barnes, an attorney at the Legal Aid Society of Northeastern New York who specializes in tenants' rights and has opposed Hooks in cases over the past year.

Under state law, tenants who fall behind on their rent must be given a three-day written or verbal warning by a landlord before an eviction proceeding can begin in court. If the judge grants a petition, the landlord must hire a process server — Hooks is one of many in the area — to deliver the petition to the tenant.

A car driven by Gaston Hooks Jr. parked in downtown Schenectady.
[Photo by Michael DeMasi]

The petition indicates when the tenant must appear in court to answer the charge. If the two sides can't resolve their differences, a trial is scheduled. The landlord or their attorney must appear before the judge.

If the tenant loses at trial, the landlord must arrange with the sheriff's department to evict the tenant. Only a sheriff's deputy has the authority to physically remove a tenant from their home.

"I get calls [from tenants who say] 'The sheriff was here,' " Barnes said. "I don't even blink."

She asks, "What did he look like?"

There is no licensing requirement or training for process servers in the state outside New York City. A person must be 18 or older, not a party to the dispute and must sign an affidavit attesting to the date and the physical features of the person who was served papers.

Hooks charges $335 to serve eviction notices, which includes filling out the paperwork, serving petitions, court fees, attending hearings and bolting the doors on an apartment after the sheriff has executed the eviction.

That compares with $99 for a soup-to-nuts eviction notice at Ideal Office Center in downtown Schenectady. In Albany, Attorneys Process and Research Service charges $40, plus a $35 court-filing fee. The Schenectady County Sheriff's Department does process service for less than $30.

Phil Chiarella, of Attorneys Process and Research Service, said the only reason for him to show up at a court hearing is if the process service is contested, which has happened to him maybe once in 30 years.

"He's pulling the wool over somebody's eyes," Chiarella said, figuring that Hooks gets a lot of work from downstate landlords accustomed to paying high fees for evictions.

Beasley Rollins, a Schenectady landlord, says he's been very satisfied with the work that Hooks has done for him.

Rollins has hired Hooks numerous times over the past four years to notarize an eviction notice and serve the papers that Rollins has filled out on his own. He said Hooks charges him only $50.

Hooks' uniform and official-looking cars don't trouble Rollins. Many people who are aware of Hooks' routine simply laugh it off, he said.

"It's obvious that he's doing something to impress people but I don't think he's impersonating anybody," Rollins said. "I don't think he's that dumb."

But Donna Gonzalez, a crisis intervention counselor at Schenectady Community Action Program, said Hooks has been known to be "very forceful and intimidating" by banging on doors, showing up late at night and parking around the corner from houses to wait for people to show up.

Hooks denies staking out properties, saying he follows a strict protocol that includes tape recording all interactions with tenants.

"A lot of tenants have no knowledge that he's not employed by any law enforcement agency," Gonzalez said. "As a former police officer myself [in Florida], I think that's very disrespectful."

Hooks allegedly stepped over the line last year with a woman named Jennifer L. Gauvreau.

On May 15, 2002, Hooks pulled up in front of her home at 31 Waldorf Place in the Vale neighborhood, shined a flashlight on her car, told Gauvreau he was a police officer and that her car was about to be towed, according to a sworn statement she signed.

Gauvreau saw what appeared to be a badge hanging around Hooks' neck, and saw him talking into what appeared to be a police radio, according to the statement. Gauvreau moved the car without further incident.

Based on the statement, city police charged Hooks with second-degree criminal impersonation, a misdemeanor.

Hooks admits to having a badge under his shirt that day identifying himself as a court process server. Hooks claims it was all a misunderstanding, and had Gauvreau sign another statement last October recanting her accusation that Hooks said he was a police officer.

Assistant District Attorney Michele Schettino has now charged Hooks with fourth-degree tampering with a witness. Hooks pleaded not guilty to both charges. The case is scheduled for trial on June 23.

Schenectady County Sheriff Harry Buffardi calls Hooks "a cop buff" and remembers 30 years ago as a young deputy writing a ticket because Hooks had red lights on his car. At the time, he said Hooks worked as a security guard at a bar in Glenville.

"He used to have all kinds of markings on a car that gave the presumption of authority," Buffardi said. "He looked very much like a deputy sheriff."

Hooks insists he drove a gray unmarked car at the time, and that Buffardi never wrote him a ticket, calling it "a damn lie." He also said he's not a cop buff.

"This is something new, court process officer," said Hooks, a 1974 Linton High School graduate who began working in the security business as a teenager. "You've got a 300-pound black guy coming at night banging on your door, people get nervous. I get out in rural areas. If you're in uniform, you look professional. People give you that respect."

Hooks has had other run-ins with the law in the past.

Two years ago, he was ordered to serve weekends in jail for five months and pay $39,000 in restitution to former clients who hired him to prepare legal documents, mostly uncontested divorce papers, at a firm he owned at the time, Justice For All Document Preparation. The work was never done.

According to the state Attorney General's Office, which prosecuted the case, Hooks served the jail sentence, but has only paid $2,933 of the restitution. The state is garnishing $75 a month from a property management contract Hooks has with a federally subsidized housing project, and is attempting to seize other assets he owns.

The process is long and difficult.

"We will continue to pursue any assets or access to accounts that may be linked to Mr. Hooks," said Paul Larabee, a spokesman for the attorney general.

Hooks no longer runs Justice For All, but he does business at the same 1001 State St. address under five different names registered with the county clerk's office, including Court Process Division and Gaston's Free Apartment Finding Services.

***

I didn't Google the name 'Gaston Hooks Jr.' when I wrote the story. Otherwise, I might have known about a Seattle Times story that was published April 11, 1991 — 12 years before mine.

The story was about two towing company owners who were facing legal problems in Seattle. One was "the somewhat legendary Gaston Hooks Jr."

The article says Hooks, then 35 years old, "used to dress like a cop, drive a police-like car, call his business 'Community Police Traffic and Parking Enforcement' agency, and will be forever remembered as the grinch who impounded the Forgotten Children's Fund Santa van on a cold and snowy day just before Christmas."

Years later, deception landed Hooks in a New York state prison.

He was found guilty in 2004 of perjury, criminal solicitation, conspiracy and tampering with physical evidence in Schenectady County.

The charges were filed when he allegedly impersonated a police officer in an attempt to have Jennifer L. Gauvreau move a parked vehicle.

He was also accused of tampering with a witness for getting Gauvreau to sign a statement — written by him — in which she recanted what happened.

He then "purportedly recruited others to give false statements and testimony at the trial regarding the criminal impersonation and witness tampering charges," according to a 2007 appeals court ruling upholding the conviction.

Hooks went to prison on December 19, 2004 and was released October 22, 2007, according to the New York State Department of Corrections and Community Supervision.

I wasn't sure what became of Hooks after he got out. I considered trying to track him down. It was easier than I imagined.

One day in June 2018 while in Schenectady I saw a black-and-white car resembling a police cruiser on State Street with the windows rolled down. I got a quick glimpse of the driver and immediately recognized Hooks. There was also a big dog with its head sticking out of a window.

The car disappeared out of view but I suspected where I would find Hooks: downtown, on the second floor of city hall, waiting to speak to a judge about an eviction.

I was partly right.

He was seated alone in the courtroom with a German shepherd at his feet when I walked in. I sat next to him and introduced myself. He said he remembered me and didn't like the story I wrote about him. He was soft-spoken and polite. We talked for about 10 minutes, and he had a ready answer for all of my questions. He told me he resumed doing evictions after getting out of prison.

"People can say what they want to say but I'm all legal," he said. "There have been no complaints. Everybody is my friend until I knock on their door. 'Oh, I didn't like that black S.O.B. anyway.' Hey, I'm sorry, pay your rent."

He said his courtroom appearance that day had nothing to do with serving evictions. He said police ticketed him for not

having a leash on his dog, Jasper. It was all because of a neigh-
bor who has a beef with him, Hooks said.

His hair was graying and I asked his age. He said 62. I
asked if he has a fascination with dressing like a cop.

"No, I just like getting the job done and getting it done pro-
fessionally," he said. "If I was a garbage man I'd be the best look-
ing, sharpest garbage man there was."

ALBANY CITY ASSESSOR ADMITS COSTLY MISTAKE

June 15, 2017

Albany Business Review

The Albany city assessor today admitted making a mistake when he granted exemptions on certain commercial properties in the city, an acknowledgment that came after *Albany Business Review* raised questions about a program that has benefited 50 properties, including luxury condos downtown.

"It was my mistake," said Keith McDonald who has been the assessor for 30 years, a tenure that began under former Mayor Thomas Whalen. "We're in the process of doing some corrections."

He attributed the mistake to a misinterpretation of one word — "and" — in Section 485-a of Real Property Tax Law. He refused to specify which properties would be affected by the corrections, or explain how long the process would take.

The corrections could have a big impact on the property taxes owed by certain property owners if the exemptions are rescinded. It's unclear if or when McDonald would take that step.

The assessor has sole discretion over the exemptions. They are not reviewed or approved by the Common Council or Mayor Kathy Sheehan.

Albany Business Review has been researching a story about the exemptions. They have become increasingly popular in Albany since they were first awarded five years ago to the owners of luxury condos at 17 Chapel downtown.

McDonald was informed by *Albany Business Review* earlier this week that state law requires commercial properties to be converted to residential *and* commercial uses in order to qualify for the exemption.

At the time, McDonald said he and the city attorneys had interpreted the law to mean the conversion could be residential *or* commercial uses.

But today he called *Albany Business Review* to say there had been a misinterpretation.

"It was one word," he said.

Of the 50 properties in Albany that receive the exemptions, including each of the 24 condos at 17 Chapel downtown, at least 27 are not, or don't appear to be, "mixed use," based on research by *Albany Business Review*.

Albany is one of 10 upstate cities that have opted in to the state law, and the only municipality in the Capital Region. Albany County and the Albany City School District also opted in, meaning property owners with the exemptions save on city, county and school taxes.

In Utica, Syracuse, Rochester, Buffalo and Niagara Falls, the exemptions were only approved when a commercial building was converted to a mixed use, as required by state law.

An example of "mixed use" would be an office or retail store on the ground floor and apartments on the upper floors.

The law doesn't require a specific percentage of residential and commercial uses, but both must be present. Commercial use is defined as "the buying, selling or otherwise providing of goods or services."

"By definition in the statute, a property cannot be totally commercial or residential to qualify," the state Department of Taxation and Finance said in a prepared statement when questioned by *Albany Business Review*. "It must be mixed use as defined in the statute."

The wording of the law is clear to other upstate assessors.

"If you read the statute, it's right there," said Michael Zazzara, the assessor in Rochester.

"That's what the law says," said David Clifford, commissioner of assessment in Syracuse.

"No doubt there has to be both elements," said Martin F. Kennedy, commissioner of the department of assessment and taxation in Buffalo.

The law is supposed to help revitalize cities by giving incentives to developers to convert warehouses, manufacturing and retail buildings into residential units and commercial uses.

The exemptions reduce the taxable assessments at a fixed amount for eight years based on the value of improvements. The exemptions then gradually phase out until the properties are taxed on the full assessment in the 13th year.

The luxury condos downtown at 17 Chapel are a prime example of how the law can generate new revenue by attracting developers to empty or under-utilized buildings — a vital need in cities like Albany.

The developer, Rosenblum Cos. converted a four-story warehouse on Chapel Street across from the Hampton Inn & Suites into a $9 million, seven-story residential building with 24 luxury condos, a rooftop terrace and a heated parking garage.

The cost savings are considerable for the condo owners. Several owners, for instance, pay $980 in total annual taxes for units that would otherwise have a tax bill of nearly $10,300.

The only "commercial" aspect of 17 Chapel is storage units that condo owners can buy or rent, and parking spaces that can be purchased. It's unclear if those fulfill the requirements of the law, since the exemptions are applied to the individual condos, not the building itself. Rosenblum Cos. referred questions to the city.

Zachary Hutchins and his wife, Kate, own one of the condos. They were renting an apartment downtown when they decided to buy the condo in 2013, paying $385,000. The exemptions on the property assessments were a major factor in their decision.

"We looked at the financials and realized for basically $100 more a month than what we were spending on rent we could own a condo in downtown Albany," said Hutchins, 34, director of communications at The Business Council of New York. "It was nicer than the apartment, and we would be building equity."

When told about McDonald's admission about making a mistake regarding the exemptions, Hutchins said, "I certainly hope the assessor recognizes the fact lots of people made decisions based upon the assessor's interpretation and that those individuals should not be punished because the assessor apparently made a mistake."

Another commercial property getting the exemptions is a former office building near the Capitol that was converted into a $10 million apartment complex called 20 Park Residences. Mayor Sheehan and other officials are scheduled to attend the grand opening of the apartments on Monday. The website for the apartments doesn't show a commercial use.

27 Western Ave. in Albany.
[Photo by Donna Abbott-Vlahos, courtesy of *Albany Business Review*]

The other properties in Albany getting the exemptions include a nine-unit apartment building at 83 Beaver St. next to Times Union Center, and a 31-unit apartment building at 27 Western Ave., a former high school annex building.

The owners of 27 Western Ave., David and Harris Sarraf, didn't return calls for comment.

Patrick Chiou, owner of 83 Beaver St., said there's no commercial use in the building. He said he wouldn't have been able to convert the building into apartments without the exemptions.

Chiou also intends to seek the exemptions on four row houses he's converting into apartments on Broadway. Those will also be strictly residential.

"I hope this doesn't open the floodgates and creates a problem," he said of the questions raised about the exemptions.

*   *   *

Here's what happened after the story ran: McDonald, the longtime assessor, immediately submitted his retirement papers; Mayor Kathy Sheehan, who was blindsided by McDonald's mistake, hired a law firm to examine the 485-a program; the law firm identified nine properties that didn't appear to qualify for the generous tax breaks; a city board ruled five of those buildings must lose the exemptions, including 27 Western Ave., costing the owners thousands of dollars; state Assemblyman John T. McDonald III sponsored a law requiring the Albany assessor to get annual training. The legislation had not reached the Assembly floor for a vote as of October 2018.

'DADDY, WHAT'S A TORNADO?'

ME VS. THE WOODCHUCK:
THE BATTLE IS OVER

July 22, 2013
Albany Business Review

Sunday, July 21, was a momentous day. It's the first time I ever trapped a wild animal. For my sake, and my neighbor's vegetable garden, I hope it's the last.

My family, friends and co-workers have been following along with my attempts to catch a woodchuck in my backyard the past six weeks. It has been both funny and frustrating.

The woodchuck, I call him Woody, was apparently living under my shed. I know this because of the dirt tracks where he dug a hole to get underneath and then another hole to exit.

I knew it was a woodchuck because I would occasionally see him frolicking in the backyard while I was looking out the kitchen window. It was as if he was saying, "Hey, nice place you have here! I think I'll stay a while."

This would not be such a big deal except for the fact Woody annihilated two of my neighbors' vegetable gardens last year.

It was so bad one neighbor didn't bother planting this year. The other forged ahead, and it soon became evident Woody was feasting again.

Just by way of background, I grew up in a city. Not *the* city. But it was an urban enough upbringing to know absolutely nothing about trapping a wild animal.

Further disclosure: I do not own a gun. Even if I did, firing one is discouraged in the middle of suburbia.

Thankfully I had the internet. Plus friends, co-workers, store employees, and acquaintances more than happy to give me advice on what to do.

Captured! [Photo by Michael DeMasi, courtesy of *Albany Business Review*]

In particular, what bait to use in my Havahart trap. Suggestions included melon rinds, lettuce, carrots, "stinky bananas," apples, apples smothered in peanut butter, and cucumbers.

I nabbed a squirrel with the melon rinds and lettuce.

I snagged a skunk with the carrots.

The bananas just withered in the heat.

I'm not sure what ate the apples, but he/she made off with the loot without tripping the cage door shut.

Out of ideas, and patience, I tried something completely different over the weekend. Instead of setting the trap near my shed, I suggested my neighbor put it in his vegetable garden. After all, that's where Woody was getting his three squares a day for free.

Boom!

Or, in this case I should say, Rattle!

We caught him after just one night.

Right now I'm sure you're wondering what bait finally did the trick.

Nothing. The trap had no bait. Why Woody ventured inside we'll never know.

We do know he has been relocated about five miles away — with the help of my neighbor's pickup truck — to live out his days in another, more rural part of town.

So long, Woody.

WHEN A TORNADO WARNING SENDS YOU TO THE BASEMENT

May 31, 2013

Albany Business Review

After more than 43 years living in the Capital Region, I'm used to unpredictable weather, but Wednesday night was the first time I found myself hunkered down in the basement wondering if a tornado would hit my home.

I'll save you the suspense and tell you even though two tornados touched down in the area [one more severe than the other], the National Weather Service says neither were in my Clifton Park neighborhood, though one touched down in Vischer Ferry, not far from where I live.

Whipping winds took down numerous trees and branches, the power was knocked out, and roads and backyards were flooded after the storm passed. For a short time, it looked like a river was flowing down my street.

My family definitely escaped the worst of it. I feel bad for the many people whose homes and property were damaged, and for the man in Mariaville who was injured. Thankfully, no one was killed.

Years from now, several experiences will stand out in my memory. Here are a few:

- Sitting at the kitchen table with my twin, 4-year-old daughters and hearing an unfamiliar sound coming from my iPhone on the counter a few feet away. It was a text from the National Weather Service that said "Tornado Warning in this area until 7:30 PM EDT. Take shelter now. Check local media."

- Trying to balance the need to stay calm while trying to get my daughters into the basement as quickly as possible. "Daddy, what's a tornado?" was a question I delicately answered after one of my daughters overheard me say the word when I called my wife to let her know what was happening. "Daddy, I have to pee" was a bit of unfortunate timing.

- Hearing the winds and holding my daughters' hands when the lights went out in the basement, briefly plunging us into darkness. Holding my breath that our household generator would kick on, as I promised the girls it would. Exhaling when the light bulb above our heads flickered to life.

- The relief I felt when it was over, and the pride for how my daughters handled everything.

- Telling myself next time — let's hope there isn't a next time — I'll remember to bring a flashlight.

[Photo by Michael DeMasi, courtesy of *Albany Business Review*]

LOST AND FOUND
AT PRICE CHOPPER

April 29, 2013

Albany Business Review

The news arrived one night last week on the answering machine at home.

A customer service manager at a local Price Chopper called to say there was something of mine at the store.

She said it had been there for a year, maybe longer, in the safe.

My mind raced: what could it be?

I called the store and explained who I was.

A few minutes later I heard this unexpected question: "Did you lose your wallet?"

The memories came flooding back: reaching for my wallet and not finding it; the frantic retracing of steps; the worrying about identity theft; and the depressing realization days later that it was gone for good.

Then, of course, the phone calls: cancelling the credit and ATM cards, getting a new driver's license, replacing my insurance cards, etc. etc.

Lots of people have experienced the same thing.

Time passes, and life moves on.

[Photo by Mike DeSocio]

I had forgotten I lost my wallet until I got the phone call.

When I went to the store to pick it up, naturally I was curious why it had taken so long to contact me.

The customer service manager said someone tried to call me after the wallet was found, but I never responded. After 30 days, the wallet was put in the store safe.

It sat there until last week, when the manager was cleaning out the safe, saw the wallet, and wondered why it was never claimed.

I have to say I don't remember getting a message from the store. If I did, I'm sure I would have immediately retrieved the wallet.

Some people would be angry about what happened. I wasn't, especially since nothing was missing, including $137 in cash [I don't usually carry that much money].

We don't know who turned it in, but obviously a good person.

As for exactly how long ago the wallet disappeared, I called Discover to ask when my current card was issued.

Answer: March 2010.

Three years and one month later, the wallet and I are having a surprise reunion.

A SALUTE TO DADS COMFORTABLE IN THEIR OWN SKIN

June 16, 2017

Albany Business Review

The first time I saw my neighbor with painted toenails was last year at the town pool. They were fluorescent orange.

I thought it was funny because Jay Raylinksy is an electrician with a barrel chest and imposing look.

I didn't ask, "Why?"

I figured it out on my own.

He's a dad with two young daughters, just like me.

His girls were with him at the pool, too.

Fathers of a certain age today understand, and accept, there are things we do to please our children that our own dads would have never done.

This was humorously demonstrated a few years ago in a movie when a dad, played by the actor Owen Wilson, sat patiently on his daughter's bed while she twisted his short hair into tight knots.

He didn't mind at all.

[Photo by Michael DeMasi, courtesy of *Albany Business Review*]

Traditionalists will scoff that parents need to act like adults, not children. I get their point, but also know occasionally looking silly keeps egos in check. The bigger man is the one who won't let the opinions of others drag him down. That's a great lesson for every kid.

My neighbor was at the town pool again this week with his daughters, this time sporting electric blue toenails.

I asked him to explain the backstory.

He told me he had them first painted when his oldest daughter went to a birthday party that his youngest daughter wasn't invited to attend. As a treat, he took her to a salon, and they both got pedicures.

A sweet tradition was born between father and daughter.

He's done it four times so far, and has no qualms about showing off the brightly colored results. He'll even wear flip-flops to the mall.

This Father's Day, when we celebrate dads of all stripes, let's add a special salute to those who demonstrate every day they're comfortable in their own skin.

And toes.

WHY YOU SHOULD PITCH A TENT IN THE YARD THIS SUMMER

June 30, 2014

Albany Business Review

An overnight trip to visit a childhood friend at one of the Finger Lakes this past weekend was a wake up call to summer:

Start enjoying it more now because, as we all know, it will go fast.

This helps explain why I woke up Sunday morning inside a tent pitched on my front lawn in Clifton Park.

I strongly suggest you do the same.

It's a calming experience that helps clear your head and slows time, two things we all could use in the daily, crazy dash to 'get stuff done.'

I bought the tent a couple of months ago after promising my twin 5-year-old daughters we would sleep outside when the weather finally turned warm.

I am not a camper by any stretch of imagination. Sure, I have hiked a few mountains, swam in state parks and fished at local ponds. But the outdoors is something I almost exclusively have experienced awake.

So I was a quarter-step beyond my comfort zone when I walked out of Dick's Sporting Goods with an $80 Coleman four-person tent slung over my shoulder in a convenient carry-all bag.

I'm assuming most people who make the same purchase do it to be ready for a trip to the woods at least a car's drive away.

I had more limited, initial ambitions: the backyard.

The time was right Saturday. I was back from Skaneateles Lake, its breathtaking beauty fresh in my mind. The weather was perfect, and the forecast the same. Our family had nowhere to be.

The girls, of course, were thrilled and started playing in and around the tent long before bedtime.

As every parent can attest, it's rare for any plan to go off without a hitch.

I ditched the backyard for the front after examining the branches overhead on our towering oak trees. There were no storms in sight, but I didn't want to end up in one of those tragic stories on the evening news because of a freak accident.

[Photo by Michael DeMasi, courtesy of *Albany Business Review*]

After the sunset and the PJs were on, one of my daughters had a change of heart at the last minute, preferring instead to sleep indoors with mom.

My other daughter wavered but chose the tent. Once settled in, she fell asleep faster than usual with the help of a book we had checked out of the library that day. A moment later, I was out cold.

This is not an earth-shattering observation, but it's worth emphasizing: you fall asleep faster outside, and wake up earlier. No digital screens or artificial lights will do that.

Here's something else: your other senses are heightened. I heard birds in the morning that seemed foreign, if not otherworldly.

There was very little traffic. The two fastest cars on our street stopped abruptly at the foot of the driveway, made a loud thud and raced off. They were the guys delivering the Sunday paper.

I'm not going to say I slept like a rock, even with an inflatable mattress separating us from the ground. But it was relaxing and fun, and a memory my other daughter will hopefully cherish.

I know I will, especially the part when my wife zipped open the tent door in the morning and said, "Good morning, campers!"

ARTISTS
AND THEIR
CANVASES

EXPRESSIONS OF LIFE:
PAINTER HARRY ORLYK

December 13, 1992

The Post-Star

The days growing up on the streets of Cohoes came back in gentle waves to Harry Orlyk, like the creek running passed his small art studio on Blind Buck Road in Salem.

To Orlyk, Cohoes was a place of beauty and wonderment. It was a place where he was always surrounded by family — Polish immigrants who worked in the meatpacking business. He could count six different buildings on the street where he was reared, each of them home to an Orlyk or Bilinski.

An industrial city north of Troy, Cohoes also had a sense of wilderness. Orlyk fished at a nearby pond. He spent time on a farm pitching hay and doing chores. He walked through the woods outside his back door.

And he watched as the land was slowly partitioned off. A large pit left by a mining company doubled as a swimming hole during the summer. Then, later in life, came housing developments.

Now 45 years old and settled into his own home with a wife and four children, Orlyk identifies with the tranquil pace that Cohoes once held. In many ways, it's a time gone by, he said. But in rural Washington County, he can still connect with nature.

"I'm paying tribute to a local humankind," he said about his expressionistic paintings. "The people who have left all these marks on the land. The stone walls. The bridges."

Harry Orlyk
[Photo by Michael DeMasi, courtesy of *The Post-Star*]

Orlyk speaks with a folksy wisdom, a straightforward, honest appraisal of his life that continually draws in the listener. Tall, with wavy brown hair and steel blue eyes, he has the physique of an outdoorsman.

On this day he was seated in a rocking chair inside the studio. There was a cast-iron stove and wide slabs of wood underfoot.

Although the cornfields and hills beyond his backyard could be a ready-made vista for his paintings, Orlyk's connection with the land most often comes from the seat of a navy blue Dodge van.

Nearly every day he climbs into what he affectionately calls his old junker, rambles to places like Hebron or Middle Falls or Easton, and parks along the side of the road. From there he finds his vantage point.

Capturing man's interaction with the environment, and lately man's involvement with man, is a passion that guides his work. When he heads out the door for the day, the headlines in the news are often the seeds of his creation. Upset or uplifted at the latest report, he'll find a scene that expresses his mood.

It may be a boy walking home, a log cutter, a cow crossing the field. They all intrigue and inspire him in some way.

His art breathes of open air and space, a soothing quality that attracts the observer. Scenes must be taken in slowly to appreciate the depth of his detail. There's just enough left out to capture the imagination.

It's a style in the vein of Dutch painter Vincent Van Gogh, one of his biggest influences.

Titles of his pieces vary between the political "Requiem for the Mothers in a Sarajevo Market" and "Prayer for the Earth Summit" to the placid "Cornfield Near the River," "Squash Harvest," and "Garden Near a Pond."

"It's evolved to a point where it's more than just finding something nice to the eye," he said. "It's evolved to something that strikes a major chord. Something that touches some part of my life."

That life is divided between hours of painting and drawing in solitude and time with his family and friends. He goes to his favorite fishing hole whenever possible, kayaks and looks forward to his regular bowling night. The diversions help keep him focused on the roughly four paintings he does weekly.

Clay sculptures are another outlet for his creativity. About two years ago he started making clay pipes in the shape of human forms, a practice he said is rooted in Native American culture. The work eventually developed into more elaborate pieces.

"They're becoming better crystallizations of my wanting to tie in with global events," he said.

A newspaper clipping showing hundreds of Haitian refugees cramped onto a boat, for instance, hangs on the wall next to a piece that depicts the misery and suffering inherent in the trip. The sculpture resembles a hollowed-out bowl with dozens of small human figurers scattered along the sides and reaching out from its depths.

"With paintings I have a tendency to want to say more, but I'm limited. I can say more with clay. There's more context that can be manipulated," he said.

One piece was inspired by the beating of Rodney King by the police in Los Angeles. Another is a "therapeutic piece" done after his mother, Olga, died.

"Mom was a ground-breaker," he said. "She was the first in her family to have children. She was the first to go back to Poland and Ukraine and visit the family."

Orlyk talks with reverence about the aunts, uncles, grandmother and other relatives who lived on his street when he was growing up. There was always somebody around to let him know his hair was out of place. And the financial security provided by his grandmother's store and the meat-packing business enabled him to explore his interests.

At age 9 Orlyk wanted to be an artist of some kind. By the time he finished high school he knew he was going to be a painter. He graduated from the State University of New York at New Paltz in 1970, and then got his master's degree from the University of Nebraska in 1974.

In Nebraska a teacher named Keith Jacobshagen introduced him to small-canvas landscape art.

"He was the person that was the counter-pole person in life," he said. Instead of being trapped in the constrictive environment of a studio, Orlyk was able to tap into the liberating feeling of being outdoors.

Today his work is displayed in galleries, homes, and businesses around the country including The Hales Gallery in Glens Falls. In November he had a show at the Venable Neslage Galleries in Washington, D.C. Another exhibition, which closed Dec. 5, was at Laighton Galleries in Schenectady.

Laighton Galleries owner Perley Laighton said Orlyk has the ability to "paint the air," a quality that relatively few artists possess.

"You can really project yourself into his work," Laighton said. "I always get the sense when I see his work that I can feel the atmosphere."

Many of his pieces are priced in the $1,000 to $2,000 range.

When he talks about his art, Orlyk goes to great lengths to describe the significance of shadows and light, of the subtle colors that lend the piece its natural feel. His relationship with the texture and mood is more palatable than some other landscape artists, he said, because he doesn't paint from a photograph.

During the winter he fights off the cold in his van with thick boots, a glove and layers of clothing. Often he'll sit in one place for hours, so taken by the scene that he dare not move. Almost by default, the dabs of paint and sweeping brush strokes become an extension of his experience at the time. A shiver can make a jagged edge that much more jagged.

These aren't things Orlyk consciously plans. Even his destinations are often the by-product of a wrong turn or missed sign. He enjoys getting lost because it means he'll see things he never before encountered.

In a way, then, the history behind each work lends it distinction. He can tell a story about "how he got that one" as much as he can explain its meaning.

When he gets as much as he can in the field, he takes the work back to the studio and puts it aside. During the following days or weeks, he goes back to study it, deciding where it needs to be strengthened and further defined. Sometimes the changes leap out at him. Other times they're less apparent.

On this day he was looking over a series of four paintings he's tentatively titled "Ways to Heaven." They include a stream cutting through the woods; a farmer walking two cows; a steel bridge set against an open field; and a father and son working on the roof of their home.

"A motif is not static," Orlyk said. "The sun moves in the sky. The wind blows. Animals and people come into the scene."

Choosing where to draw the lines around the scene is one step in the process. Although the windshield of his van helps to confine the action, its borders don't necessarily make up the edges of the picture. He has to identify the most important element and work out from there.

Tunnel vision doesn't suit a landscape artist well.

"It's important to start as loosely as possible and hone in on what it's going to be," he said.

It's especially important he stay in tune with his motivation for the painting. If a story on the morning TV news sets him off, he has to maintain that intensity. If his mood changes during the course of a sitting, it's likely to be reflected in some way on the canvas.

Over time, the painting will accept his preconceived notion. He's in touch with what he wants to say and how he wants to say it.

"I'm looking for moments that heighten the statement," he said. "The notion surrounding that day."

*   *   *

Harry Orlyk is now 71. He continues to paint rural landscapes and exhibit his work.

"It's becoming more and more the core of my energy, and my reason to want to get up and live out every day," he told me during a phone call in June 2018.

It was the first time we had spoken in 26 years. I had forgotten what his voice sounds like, but his appreciation for the natural world resonated with me.

"It's exciting to follow the seasons as intimately as I do," he said. "The seasons don't just have weather with snow in the winter and sunshine in the summer. There are all these gradations of color and light."

He still drives into the country to capture the scene beyond his windshield, but finally traded up four years ago from a rusty van. "I bought a brand new Ford with a dynamite engine," he said. "I have a lot of confidence in it when I park in these long winter painting sessions."

He wonders what he would do if his eyesight starts failing. But his vision remains good. And he stays busy in other ways: bowling with friends, playing harmonica, writing a journal and mentoring young artists.

"I hope I'm not tempting the great maker right now," he said. "I'm really blessed."

INSIDE ALBANY'S COLD STORAGE BUILDING

December 14, 2017

Albany Business Review

"Step into my office."

Evan Blum said the words with his usual quiet, understated humor. He had just unlocked a door and we were walking into the old Central Warehouse in north Albany, a wreck of a building that's been an ugly landmark on the city's horizon for decades.

I had been looking forward to this moment for the past several weeks, since I first contacted Blum's head of business development, Ann Sklar, at his business, Demolition Depot & Irreplaceable Artifacts, in Harlem.

Here was the proposal: I would travel downstate to meet him in person and talk about his plans for the building that he bought in August for $280,357.

In exchange, he would come to Albany to give me a tour of the 11-story concrete fortress that thousands of people see daily while driving on Interstate 787, but which relatively few have seen from the inside.

The only visitors, if you can call them that, were those desperate for refuge on an Albany winter's night or who wanted to spray paint graffiti; get high; strip anything valuable that could be sold as scrap; surreptitiously take pictures, or do who-knows-what.

The floors were once full of workers unloading frozen food and dry goods from train cars and trucks, storing the products, and then loading everything into smaller trucks and vans bound for grocery stores in the region.

Now it's as if time itself had frozen.

"Truck Driver's Lounge" reads a sign in the shipping and receiving area. "No Drivers Beyond White Line," says another.

Graffiti of every imaginable color and design is scrawled on the walls. A thick layer of dirt covers the floor, along with broken glass and debris: a box of Glad garbage bags; a Mr. Subb soda cup; an empty 12-pack carton of Milwaukee's Best; a twisted bicycle wheel; a toilet bowl seat.

There's a wide-open mechanical pit with standing water at the bottom, where a full-size plastic Santa Claus lays prone. It's one of many sights, such as the nearly 40-year-old purchase orders and petty cash receipts strewn about a room on an upper floor. Elsewhere, a pair of rumpled blue jeans.

The light is surprisingly bright in parts of the building, and the air has no discernible smell, no doubt because the wind blows through the broken windows.

I was there with our photographer, Donna Abbott-Vlahos, and digital editor, Mike DeSocio, who was shooting video.

Blum asked that we not focus so much on the ruins. He wants people to envision how the space can be reborn.

I've learned he isn't some naive optimist. He's an expert appraiser of architectural artifacts and a hard-working, successful business owner with 40 years of experience finding value in old things.

Run-down buildings don't intimidate him. It's people that make his work challenging.

"Dealing with inanimate objects is less daunting to me than the moving ones," he likes to say.

Evan Blum outside the former Central Warehouse cold storage building [Photo by Donna Abbott-Vlahos, courtesy of *Albany Business Review*]

Still, as we climbed the crumbling concrete staircase to the roof and gawked at the view, I couldn't help but think this reclamation project was going to be much harder and costlier than Blum anticipates.

The building has been without electricity, heat, and running water for many years, perhaps decades. There are no elevators. Many windows are shattered or missing, including those at knee-high level on the narrow staircase landings, an obvious safety hazard.

I wondered about any environmental cleanup that might be required.

In 2007, the Department of Environmental Conservation received a report commissioned by the real estate investors who owned the property at the time. Based on the report, the DEC said there are no significant issues that required immediate action, although the agency noted the environmental assessment was done without DEC's oversight or involvement.

As for asbestos, the state Department of Labor has no records of any work being done at the building, so it's unclear whether there's material that must be removed. If so, the cost will be considerable.

Blum isn't oblivious to the obstacles ahead, and he's accustomed to skepticism.

"When people don't see your vision, you get a variety of reactions," he said. "From comic disbelief to 'hmmm, I didn't think of that' or 'you're crazy.'"

I had to ask him one more question as we stood on the second floor where train cars used to pull inside the building. The tracks are now gone, the steel removed at some point for its scrap value. The area feels like a phantom New York City subway station.

Blum is 63-years-old. He's never been married, has no children and no apparent successor to his business. What will happen, I tried to delicately say, if he's not able to accomplish his goals at the cold storage building before he's gone, too?

He paused briefly before answering.

"I hope it's not going to take that long."

*　*　*

As of October 2018, the cold storage building was still a big, ugly landmark along the main highway into Albany. Evan Blum has removed the broken windows, secured the building to keep out vagrants and talked to local officials about his ideas, including wrapping the exterior with a giant ad to generate income to pay for improvements. He told me he's determined to get the work done. Ultimately, it will take lots of money, the city's cooperation and Blum's commitment to rescue the industrial relic.

MURALIST TRANSFORMS
CHURCH'S GYM WALLS

January 1, 2000

The Daily Gazette

The paint brush in Claude Seward's hand glided gently over the cheek of a young boy, applying flesh tone to the wall mural one stroke at a time.

Sitting on a wood-plank scaffold, Seward tried to concentrate on the task before him and shut out the sounds of children playing on the gym floor 15 feet below.

In the more than three years he has been creating a mural in the gymnasium at State Street Presbyterian Church, Seward has adapted to the shrieks of laughter and rattle of metal grates that occasionally fill the room.

"What are you going to do?" Seward said. "You live with it. They're just little kids. I have five kids of my own. I'm accepting of their foibles."

The at-risk youth attend a weekday program at the church run by Northeast Parent & Child Society. The gym is a place for eating lunch and exercising muscles and lungs.

The children have grown accustomed to the paint-splattered scaffold pushed against a wall, and the artist perched above with his brushes, bottles of paint, paper cups and other supplies.

All around are the fruits of Seward's labor: a panorama of lush greens, brilliant reds, misty blues and sparkling yellows.

Statue-sized depictions of the apostles John, Luke, Mark and Matthew hold forth on one wall. Trees, birds, arched columns and a water fountain grace another.

Scenes evoking Schenectady's skyline — the Nott Memorial, City Hall, First Presbyterian Church and St. John the Evangelist — anchor the third wall, the one presently occupying Seward's attention as he nears completion.

"The east wall I treated as the sunrise wall," Seward, 66, explained. "The south as mid-morning. The north as mid-afternoon and the west as sunset. So, we can legitimately say we invite people to stay the whole day no matter how long they stay in the cloister."

Cloisters — a covered walkway or arched path meant for solitude and reflection — are often found inside monasteries. That's the image that came to mind when Seward began thinking about the mural several years ago.

He first came to the church in 1994 when his friend, Helen Dejnozka, the organist, asked his advice on how best to remove layers of green paint from the sanctuary walls.

A muralist and retired art professor living at the time in the Saratoga County hamlet of Rock City Falls, Seward had extensive knowledge of paints and colors. He soon took charge of the sanctuary restoration, overseeing the selection of colors and creating stencils to match the patterns of the stained glass windows.

"Claude just took over," marveled the Rev. Robert Smith. "What a gift."

With the help of volunteers, including prisoners from Mount McGregor in Wilton, in three months the sanctuary was transformed from a drab room to a spectacular house of worship that closely mirrors the original appearance of 1896.

The Hall of Murals at State Street Presbyterian Church
[Photo by Michael DeMasi]

The improvement lifted the spirits of a congregation whose membership has dwindled since the days of peak General Electric employment in Schenectady a half-century ago, Smith said.

After finishing the sanctuary restoration, Seward and Smith talked about the gym, a place that once hosted packed basketball games and church tournaments.

Seward then left on a trip to Egypt.

"I thought this place has a lot of potential for community outreach, but I'm not sure the focus of outreach is basketball," said Smith, who has been pastor for 10 years.

"There's got to be a dozen basketball courts in the city," Smith remembers thinking. "Why do we have to maintain a pink gym with no windows?"

Seward asked Smith to take pictures of the 23-foot-high gym walls and mail them to him in Egypt. There, he sketched out the scenes of the cloister on paper.

He returned to the United States. On Oct. 31, 1996, he and Smith started the arduous process of sealing over the cement block walls with a bonding material.

Bit by bit, Seward began painting the mural. An anonymous donor paid for the paints and other supplies. Seward works for free.

Now divorced, he lives in Niskayuna.

Nearly every day for the past three-plus years, Seward has arrived at the gymnasium in the late morning and remained until early evening, painstakingly bringing his vision to life.

Smith wants to use the gym for banquets, entertainment and gatherings — a way to better unite the people who live in the Vale neighborhood, one of the poorest sections of the city.

In addition to the mural, the room will be spruced up thanks to a curtain being made for the stage. The combination auditorium/gym hasn't had curtains since it was built in 1956. Smith also hopes to raise money to replace the fluorescent lights.

The mural has been a therapy of sorts for Seward, who underwent an operation in the early 1970s to remove a blood clot from his brain. He had to learn to speak again. He appears fully recovered, though his speech isn't as fluid as he would like it to be.

Seward hopes to finish the mural by March, but isn't faced with any deadlines. He takes his time, examining the scene before him, dabbing his brush in a plastic container top that serves as a makeshift palette.

"The problem is always with this paint that it dries darker in value and you never know definitively what color you've got," he said.

* * *

Claude Seward finished the murals at the State Street Presbyterian Church on July 7, 2000, about seven months after my story was published.

I didn't step foot inside the old gymnasium/auditorium again until May 2018 when I contacted the church asking if I could see the paintings. An elder, Mark Sturtevant, was happy to show me around.

"How many people have something like this?" Sturtevant said as we stood looking at the large, colorful images on the upper portion of three walls. "It was a labor of love."

Folding tables and chairs were set up on the floor. On the walls below the murals were signs for community events, a food pantry and various outreach programs. A men's homeless group meets regularly there.

A bulletin board near the gym has a folder with information about "The Hall of Murals." Seward had typed three double-sided pages explaining his inspiration and rationale behind every person and building.

"The Apostle, Mark, was awed when Jesus healed the lame and raised the dead, among other miracles," Seward wrote. "Mark is seen as 'orant,' or asking prayerfully, on behalf of the afflicted that their misery be ended. The light descending on Mark's countenance indicates a possible response."

Curtains hung on the auditorium stage. They were another improvement that the former pastor, the Rev. Robert Smith, oversaw. He wasn't able to replace the long rows of fluorescent bulbs on the ceiling before he retired, but the murals soften the bright light.

Sturtevant pointed out a detail that made me smile. The face of the apostle Luke resembles that of Seward.

I don't know if the artist did that because he especially admired Luke or if it was just a wink of the eye from a man who was full of life.

I can't ask because Seward died on Valentine's Day 2014. He was 80 years old.

ALL POLITICS
IS LOCAL

CONSTANTINO ENDS TUMULTUOUS TENURE

December 31, 1997

The Daily Gazette

A student of politics since the early '70s when he campaigned door-to-door for his father, James A. Constantino knew he would have a tough time getting re-elected Rotterdam town supervisor this year.

So tough, that the longest-tenured officeholder in Schenectady County — nine consecutive years as a councilman and 13 years as supervisor — considered very seriously not running.

But a combination of factors — pride, his ego, and the belief voters would look past the most recent two years of controversies — convinced Constantino to take another stab at the $16,000-per-year, part-time job.

He failed miserably, along with the other Democratic candidates for Town Board.

All were defeated by Republicans in November.

Constantino's loss ended, at least for now, a political career in which new businesses replaced old on Altamont Avenue and other commercial strips; water and sewer systems were improved; highway equipment was upgraded; Rotterdam Square mall was built; water rates were kept low and housing cul-de-sacs sprouted like daisies.

Longtime friends and associates say Constantino's legacy will be that of a hard-working, accessible supervisor who encouraged economic growth, boosted youth sports programs and devoted much of his life to a town that welcomes visitors with windmill-shaped road signs declaring it "A Nice Place to Live."

"He lived, ate and slept what he could do for the town of Rotterdam," said Councilman Vincent T. Fernandez, who has known Constantino for about 30 years. Fernandez will be the only Democrat on the Town Board next year; his term was not up this year.

"There was not a function he would not attend," Fernandez added. "There's not a 50th wedding anniversary he didn't know about. He went to all the wakes, and involved himself in many, many activities."

In 1993, Constantino was recognized by a statewide government association for his work to protect Schenectady County's source of drinking water, an honor that many of his critics would scoff at today because of his support for a new landfill off Rynex Corners Road.

His legion of detractors says his administration was marked by poor fiscal management; a growing debt load; a 24 percent tax increase in 1997; putting the needs of developers ahead of longtime residents, and vindictiveness toward his opponents.

Even with all those new homes that were built, the town's population shrank by about 3 percent between 1980 and 1995, according to the Capital District Regional Planning Commission.

The decrease can be attributed to the decline in the average household size, as smaller families occupied homes and the population grew older, according to the town's 1993 comprehensive master plan.

Tax rates have fluctuated in the last five to 10 years. In 1997, the owner of an average home paid about $326 in town taxes, not including special district fees, such as for sewer, water and fire service. That compares with $244 in 1992 and $286 in 1987.

To know Constantino, 52, is to understand that he's a study in contrasts.

He talks with sincerity about his concern for the fate of his hometown, from which he has never strayed far. He played in Rotterdam Little League and Babe Ruth, graduated from the University at Albany and has worked as a social studies teacher in Mohonasen High School since 1968.

A man who laughs easily and enjoys talking to people — especially, it seems, when he campaigns door-to-door — Constantino possesses several of the qualities voters look for in a local politician: a nice guy who is accessible with deep roots in town.

"He answered every constituent's complaint [and] always returned calls," said Frank E. O'Connor, who served alongside Constantino as deputy supervisor for 11 years. "He never said no to anyone insofar as trying to help them out."

But during his tenure Constantino also often found himself trying to shake off charges of corruption, sweetheart deals for developers and political shenanigans, like the accusation in September that he recruited high school graduates to register with the Right-to-Life Party in a last-minute bid to win a primary [he denies doing so].

He made a lot of enemies in the northern, rural part of town, where Rotterdam ran a dump for 20 years and a private company plans to build a new, 33-acre landfill.

Constantino can get riled up easily, and, like many other politicians, feels singled-out and persecuted by the press.

At times after the November election, he seemed to relish the myriad problems that will be left in his successor's lap, though he denies this, too.

"I leave with mixed emotions," Constantino said during a recent interview in his office at Town Hall. "I know I'm leaving the town with a tremendous amount of problems. I'm relieved I don't have to handle [them] but am still concerned. I wish I had a chance to stay and work them out."

Constantino earned a lot of political mileage by teaching at Mohonasen. The job, along with his ties to the town Democratic

Committee, formed a support base that helped propel him to his first electoral victory.

In February 1975, he was appointed by Democrats to fill a vacancy on the Town Board. That November, he won his first four-year term as councilman. At the time his father, Al, was the town clerk; he died in 1976.

In 1984, Constantino was elected in a special election to succeed John "Bud" Kirvin as supervisor.

Kirvin, a politician for more than 25 years, was legendary. He collapsed at the start of a live TV debate, dying four days before the 1983 election. His name still appeared on the ballot, however, and he won 70 percent of the vote.

"Dead Man Wins Re-Election," was the headline on a UPI story.

After becoming supervisor Constantino went on to win six more races — one of them, in 1993, by only 104 votes.

In recent years, Constantino seemed to lose credibility with the public. A state audit covering an 18-month period in 1994 and 1995 found numerous deficiencies in how the town was being run, including awarding contracts without seeking competitive bids, questionable cellular phone calls and insufficient oversight of the budget.

Last June, the state Comptroller's Office offered to help straighten out financial problems, such as general fund deficits three of the last four years, but Constantino declined, saying the situation was under control.

Marjorie Schmid of Schermerhorn Road, a longtime critic of Constantino, characterized his tenure as one of "accelerated commercial growth with no long-range planning."

Schmid, who fought unsuccessfully for 12 years to stop Rotterdam Square Mall from being built, regularly attends Town Board meetings.

Constantino often refers derisively to Schmid and others who criticize him as "wing nuts."

"He went through wannabe, a whiner and wing nut," Schmid said. "I told him his alliteration was marvelous, but could he start at another letter?"

Some of the loudest voices speaking out against Constantino over the last two years have been residents of the Pattersonville hamlet, where the town once ran a municipal dump. A private company, Capital Waste & Recycling of Albany, plans to build a 33-acre construction and demolition debris landfill.

Perhaps more than anything else, the town's foray into a new landfill business resulted in the negative publicity that several officials say hurt Constantino in the election.

When it comes to the landfill, Constantino said he was in a no-win situation politically.

With the closing of the municipal dump in 1994, he had to cut services drastically, raise taxes or try to replace $2 million in revenue that had been collected in tipping fees. He chose the latter, and the town signed a contract with New Options on Waste to run a small construction and demolition debris landfill off Rynex Corners Road.

But the town ran into financial and environmental problems at the new landfill that resulted in budget shortfalls and state fines.

In retrospect, Constantino said many mistakes were made during his tenure, including signing a contract with New Options on Waste to build the landfill [the company has since been bought by Capital Waste] and giving the cold shoulder to landfill opponents.

Some say privately that Constantino also suffered politically because of the personal relationship he had with the town zoning officer, Michele Wickham, while he was separated from his wife. Constantino said his divorce was finalized a few months ago.

Constantino disagrees with those who say Wickham was the reason for his downfall, and credited her for doing good work for the town. He said his biggest problem with voters was the perception the town wasn't being run properly.

"I think in the last two years, I was perceived by the public, whether right or wrong, as not doing the job they wanted. The public, for many years under the Democratic administrations, whether Kirvin or mine, perceived that everything was fine in River City."

Constantino said one of his biggest regrets was not being able to do the job on a full-time basis. Most days he arrived in the office around 3 p.m., after school let out. He called the salary an "absolute joke."

As for the future, he plans to sit back and watch the new administration for the first few months. He doesn't plan to run for supervisor again in 1999, but isn't bowing out of politics.

"I am going to stay very active in the Democratic Party and evaluate where I am six months [and] a year from now," he said.

*   *   *

The whispers about James Constantino's allegedly shady behavior as Rotterdam town supervisor turned out to be true.

In 2001 he pleaded guilty to extorting $8,000 from a local gravel company while he was supervisor in 1996, according to The Daily Gazette. He served 18 ½ months in federal prison and at a halfway house.

BRIAN STRATTON HOPES TO BE HIS OWN MAN

October 5, 2003

The Daily Gazette

It was a Friday night in the Stratton household, and 7-year-old Alex was sitting at the dining room table, excitedly pushing chess pieces across the board and loudly talking above his father.

"Blah, blah, blah," Alex said as Brian U. Stratton explained to a reporter why he made his first run for elected office a dozen years ago.

Stratton's patience all but ran out, and he called to his wife, Lisa, in the next room for help with their only child.

The Strattons have grown accustomed to Alex's high-energy and obsessive tendencies, and talk to him in a loving but direct way. Still, it's a challenge being the parents of a boy who suffers from Asperger's syndrome, a form of autism.

The couple said it was probably most stressful three years ago, when Brian, then a city councilman, spent many nights away from home campaigning in Fulton and Montgomery counties, trying to unseat longtime Republican state Sen. Hugh T. Farley.

Stratton beat Farley in Schenectady — a sign of his vote-gathering power — but lost to the longtime senator in the heavily Republican district.

Today, with the help of speech pathologists in the city school district and a greater understanding of Alex's condition, the Strattons seem ready for the rigors of balancing home life with the hectic schedule of a mayoral campaign.

It's a race that, for Brian, is filled with nearly constant reminders of his deceased father, Samuel S. Stratton, who was mayor of Schenectady from 1956 to 1958 and then served for 30 years in Congress.

Samuel Stratton distinguished himself through his support of the military during the Cold War, and attended to the needs — big and small — of his constituents back home. The Air National Guard base in Scotia and the Veterans Affairs hospital in Albany are both named for him, a testament to his legacy.

Barely a door gets knocked on in this city without someone telling Brian Stratton a wistful story about his dad. Brian said it was frustrating at the beginning of his political career because he was trying to make a name for himself.

Now 47 years old, he has grown to appreciate what his father accomplished. He can even laugh at being mistakenly called "Sam" by people who should know better, such as former state Comptroller H. Carl McCall.

"I've become more and more proud to be his son," Stratton said.

Still, living under his father's shadow has meant contending with the accusations that he's riding a legend's coattails into the election booth. Even some in his own party say there's little to his candidacy, or past accomplishments, but the last name with the golden touch.

"Stratton has no administrative ability or experience," said one Democratic insider. "He's never held a meaningful private sector job, if any."

Others see things differently.

William M. Murphy, a longtime family friend whom Brian calls "Uncle Bill," managed Samuel Stratton's first election campaign. He said Brian, like his father, is "very intelligent, very smart," and has the backbone to withstand the pressures of being mayor.

Stratton has managed to carve out an identity through some of the stances he's taken.

As a city councilman he advocated a 21 percent penalty on delinquent taxpayers. He joined other Democrats in calling for the ouster of former Police Chief Gregory T. Kaczmarek during an unfolding police corruption scandal. He pressed Mayor Albert P. Jurczynski to bring in state troopers to combat a wave of violent crime.

Brian Underhill Stratton was born Sept. 6, 1957, the youngest of Sam and Joan Stratton's five children. The family lived on Spruce Street in Schenectady and moved to Bethesda, Md., when Brian was 6 years old.

Brian began stuttering at a young age and underwent extensive speech therapy at the Hollins Communications Research Institute in Roanoke, Va., a nationally recognized treatment center. He periodically takes refresher courses. His stuttering tends to flare up in stressful situations.

"I have good days and bad days," he said. "There are challenging moments."

He attended Maryland public schools and got a two-year community college degree before transferring to SUNY Oswego, where he majored in communications and broadcasting and got a bachelor's degree in 1979.

Stratton's father, who had a brief stint as a TV and radio commentator in the early 1950s, urged his son to get into radio. Although it seems like an odd choice for a man who stutters, Stratton said it gave him a chance to tackle his speech problems head on.

He moved back to Schenectady in 1981 and worked at WRGB-TV writing advertising copy, but returned to Washington about four years later for a job in General Electric Co.'s federal lobbying office. He got bored and eventually came back to the Capital Region, settling in Clifton Park in 1986.

He lived there five years while he worked at the New York State Science and Technology Foundation, a state agency. During that time a long-term relationship with a woman ended, and his father died on Sept. 13, 1990.

The events forced him to re-examine his life.

He moved back to Schenectady in 1991 at the urging of friends and ran successfully for City Council. He won easily, and cruised to victory in two subsequent elections. He rebounded from his defeat to Farley in 2000 by winning a seat on the county Legislature a year later.

Stratton now works as director of correspondence for New York State Senate Minority Leader David Paterson, a job that puts him in Albany on a daily basis but also offers the flexibility to run a campaign and hold news conferences in Schenectady.

At the time of his first campaign he was dating the former Lisa Coppola, whom he met when he hired her for a job with the state. They married aboard a cruise ship in February 1994 and bought a house on DeCamp Avenue, just steps from the main entrance to Central Park.

These days they share the cozy, four-bedroom cottage with Alex, two cats and a rescued greyhound named Cleo.

Lisa Stratton, a spokeswoman at Union College, said her husband has a goofy sense of humor — he does halfway decent impressions of Richard Nixon and Ronald Reagan and is a snack fiend.

He loves Cheez-Its and can crunch through three to four boxes of cereal a week.

"We joke about having a grain silo in back," Lisa said.

*　　*　　*

Brian Stratton ran against Peter Guidarelli for mayor in 2003 and won by only 300 votes. Four years later Stratton crushed a different opponent to win a second term.

He experienced the thrill of his political life in January 2011 while visiting Washington, D.C. for a national mayor's conference. President Obama happened to be flying to Schenectady to give a speech at the General Electric Co. manufacturing plant.

Stratton was invited to the Oval Office and walked with Obama across the South Lawn to the Marine One helicopter, a scene captured by photographers. Obama invited Stratton to sit next to him on the helicopter during the short ride to Andrews Air Force Base to board Air Force One for the flight north.

Stratton excitedly relayed what happened in an interview with Paul Grondahl of The Times Union:

"Stratton mentioned how he and his son, Alex, might make a road trip to watch the Mets play the Chicago Cubs at Wrigley Field. Obama raved about the ballpark. They discussed the movie 'The King's Speech' and Stratton mentioned efforts to overcome his own stuttering. Obama noted that Vice President Joe Biden struggled with stuttering as a boy."

The once-in-a-lifetime opportunity came just a month before Gov. Andrew Cuomo nominated Stratton to run the state's canal system.

Stratton, who hadn't yet announced whether he would run for a third term, resigned as mayor to become director of the Canal Corp., a position he still holds. He and Lisa are no longer married.

MAYOR LEAVES RECORD OF STRUGGLE IN TRYING TIMES

December 14, 2003
The Daily Gazette

On Friday afternoon, as he has done countless times over the past eight years, Mayor Albert P. Jurczynski stood before a nervous man and woman in City Hall and asked them to repeat after him.

A moment later, after the groom fumbled with the ring, Jurczynski pronounced the couple husband and wife.

The marriage ceremony is one of the official duties carried out by the mayor's office that Jurczynski thoroughly enjoys. The smiling bride and groom were captured on a Polaroid, one of hundreds that the mayor has snapped and carefully tucked into a photo album for safekeeping.

"Can I give you a hug?" Jennifer Allen, the bride, asked excitedly.

Jurczynski happily obliged, saying it's not something many people ask him to do these days.

As he prepares to step down in two weeks after two terms in office, Jurczynski does not experience the warm embrace of the public as often as he once did.

That's likely because he has presided over some of the most tumultuous events in city history, from a corruption scandal that brought shame and dishonor to the police department to a fiscal crisis that has dropped the municipal credit rating to the lowest level in the state.

The double dose of bad news helped bring an end to Jurczynski's 20-year career in public office, as he opted not to seek a third term. It may have been too much for the Republican Party to overcome at the polls in a city dominated by Democrats.

Brian U. Stratton, whose campaign was built largely around trying to link his opponent, Peter J. Guidarelli, to Jurczynski's record, will be sworn in Jan. 1 as the first Democratic mayor in 12 years. As they were during Jurczynski's tenure, Democrats will remain firmly in control of the City Council.

Jurczynski will take a $90,000 job as first deputy director of the Governor's Office for Small Cities, a position many see as a reward for his years of loyalty to Republican Gov. George E. Pataki.

The circumstances under which Jurczynski leaves office are a far cry from what he pledged would happen when he took his first oath on Jan. 1, 1996.

In his inaugural speech on the stage of Proctor's Theatre that day, he promised to end the string of deficits that had plagued city government in the early 1990s, stop the political bickering and nurse the "once-magnificent" Schenectady back to financial health.

While it's clear those goals weren't accomplished, Jurczynski does point to other ways in which he believes the city has changed for the better: the closing of strip clubs and refurbishment of City Hall; the construction of downtown office buildings and streetscape improvements; establishing a working relationship with the governor's office; and the increase in housing values largely caused by the relocation of many Guyanese and other West Indians from New York City, an influx he aggressively encouraged.

"When I took office I inherited a city that was rapidly declining," Jurczynski said. "Too often, you turned on your water tap and the water ran brown. That is both an actual occurrence as well as a symbolic event. We fixed the city's water infrastructure and improved its streets and sidewalks."

History will be the ultimate judge of his tenure. Opinions vary on whether Jurczynski, 47, is leaving the city better or worse off than it was in 1996.

"I think it's better left unsaid," said one neighborhood leader who, like some other residents, didn't want to be identified. "Things aren't good in this city, and they haven't been good for a long time."

"Overall, I think it's about the same," said Bill Healy, owner of Bibliomania, a small bookstore on Jay Street downtown that has survived for 22 years by catering to fans of used, rare and out-of-print books. "Some things improved. Other things aren't as good as they were before."

Cathy Lewis, the sole Republican on the City Council and a legislator who doesn't toe the party line, said, "From the standpoint of trying to turn the city around from a physical improvement and economic base, I think he's leaving it better. But from a financial standpoint we're clearly in worse shape."

"Right now everything looks so bad, but much has been done," said Dolores Hutton, president of Schenectady United Neighborhoods, upon whom Jurczynski recently bestowed the city's highest civic honor, the Patroon award. "I like to look back and know he started his first four years with real determination and gusto and know his intentions were good. I'm hoping that history will look at him a little kinder."

City Council President Frank Maurizio, a Democrat, said the mayor didn't cooperate enough with the council and good ideas "would die on the vine" solely because they didn't come from the administration or one of its allies.

Overall, though, Maurizio sees more positive than negative in the mayor's legacy.

"I look to downtown and I look to a new segment of our community [the Guyanese] taking root," Maurizio said. "Overall he's leaving us better off, but he's also leaving us with tremendous challenges that we've got to deal with."

Jurczynski prided himself on running the city of 61,000 people and overseeing a $55 million general fund budget without a paid deputy, but the demands of the job seemed to overwhelm him at times.

He stopped seeing people inside his private office in City Hall after it became deluged with stacks of paper. He was habitually late signing personnel change orders to the point where many appointments were made official months after the person started on the job.

His management style could be harsh. "Governing by scream" was how one subordinate described it. He also swears. A lot. But he's careful not to embarrass himself publicly with his salty tongue.

That hard edge obscures the fact Jurczynski can crack up an audience with his self-deprecating humor and big, hearty laughs. He loves to tell stories about growing up on Wylie Street in Hamilton Hill and will show anyone who asks how to correctly fold a newspaper to achieve maximum throwing accuracy. He learned the skill from his days delivering the Gazette, a route he didn't give up until 1984, nine months into his first term as a city councilman. He was 27 years old.

"He put his heart and soul into this for eight years," said a City Hall staff member. "He worked 80 hours a week. Everybody asked him to come to everything. I think he did that. I think he should have put on a suit a couple more times, but I think he got tired."

He has attended very few City Council meetings over the past two years, saying he had grown weary of the verbal abuse from some residents. His absence has not lessened the criticism of the administration.

During his tenure, Jurczynski has had to contend with forces that were beyond his control, such as the continual decline in good-paying private sector jobs that have dealt a severe blow to many upstate cities.

The shrinking tax base caused revenues to stagnate or fall at a time when expenses, particularly police salaries, benefits and legal bills, skyrocketed. The result was multi-million dollar deficits and a harsh audit from the state Comptroller's Office in fall 2002 that the City Council didn't learn about until two months after it was released to Jurczynski.

Jurczynski has said the City Council shares the blame for the fiscal problems, blasting what he calls the "bogus" budgets that were approved over the years. In retrospect, he said, he should have vetoed more of them.

Violent crime also intensified in the city as the drug trade flourished in parts of Hamilton Hill, Vale and other neighborhoods where too many houses are abandoned or owned by absentee landlords. There have been eight homicides this year, one short of tying the all-time record, although not all of the murders can be tied to drug trafficking.

Fred Clark, first vice president of the local chapter of the NAACP, blames Jurczynski for not taking action when civil rights leaders told the mayor and former Police Chief Gregory T. Kaczmarek about allegations police officers were beating up suspects and shaking down drug dealers.

The FBI launched an investigation in the summer of 1999 that resulted in four officers going to federal prison for abusing their power to arrest drug dealers, including rewarding street informants with drugs. A separate, ongoing federal investigation is looking into whether officers routinely violated the civil rights of citizens over a four-year period.

A preliminary report released last April by the U.S. Justice Department's Civil Rights Division found systemic problems with training and procedures within the Police Department.

"I blame the mayor for the federal investigation coming about because it could have been kept in-house if he had chosen to do something about it when we first came to him," said Clark, who is also a Democratic committeeman.

Jurczynski responded: "Fred Clark is wrong. We asked the NAACP for witnesses to step forward and file reports regarding the rumors of shaking down drug dealers. We got none. Fred is also wrong that we could have kept it in-house. The breakdown of management control and accountability spread over years of bad contracts was so pervasive that only outside intervention was the right thing to do."

It took a few years, but public pressure from the scandal led Jurczynski to ask Kaczmarek to step down as chief. Jurczynski also hired a civilian commissioner to oversee the department, a move that some residents and elected Democrats had pressed him to do.

For the first time in more than 75 years, a police chief from outside the department was appointed to lead the force.

Through it all, Jurczynski said he only has two regrets about his tenure: his proposal in 1996 to merge city and county governments wasn't seriously pursued and he wasn't able to win support for a 2000 referendum that would have changed the basic structure of city government.

"The city is far better off than it was in 1996," Jurczynski said. "We have weathered the storm of thousands of GE layoffs and have begun the process of rebuilding. While it remains incomplete, it has been a substantial beginning of rejuvenation."

* * *

Al Jurczynski kept busy after he stepped down as mayor of Schenectady.

He worked for about three years in the administration of then-Gov. George Pataki, a fellow Republican.

Pataki chose not to run for a fourth term and was replaced by a Democrat, Eliot Spitzer.

That sent political appointees such as Jurczynski in search of new employment. He landed at the Montgomery County Jail as a corrections officer. The job meant he could continue accruing time in the state pension system.

He also started selling cars at a Ford dealership. He did well, but lasted just six months because working two jobs was hurting his health.

He retired from the jail in 2013 but didn't slow down. This is a man, after all, who delivered the Gazette newspaper well into his 20s and resumed the route for exercise when he was no longer mayor.

His latest gig: Uber driver.

Jurczynski told me he likes the freedom of driving when he wants, and tells passengers stories about his days as mayor.

He takes pride in the fact he served 20 consecutive years in office, the first 12 years on the city council. He was a successful Republican in a Democratic town.

"I was never a real hard line partisan," he said. "The Democrats hated me. The Republicans didn't know what to do with me."

All that time in politics rubbed off on his son, Alex, who ran for city council in 2016 as a Republican. He was just 25, but his dad had proved it possible to win in 1983 when he became the youngest person ever — 27 — elected to the council [the feat was topped in 1993 by another Republican, Peter Guidarelli, who was 26].

Alex, however, couldn't overcome the huge enrollment advantage Democrats have in Schenectady. He lost to a businesswoman, Karen Zalewski-Wildzunas, who coincidentally lives just a few doors away from the Jurczynskis.

JORDAN MAKES MARK
ON CITY POLITICS

February 20, 2005

The Daily Gazette

As chief of staff for Mayor Brian U. Stratton, Sharon Jordan stays on top of everything, including the recipe for oatmeal raisin cookies that a certain powerful Democrat loves to gobble up whenever he's in town.

"They're my Senator Schumer cookies," Jordan, 63, said cheerfully last week when a visitor to her corner office in City Hall spied a small plastic tub full of treats on her desk.

Charles Schumer, New York's senior senator, was nowhere in site this day.

But Jordan has been around local politics and government long enough to realize that a fresh-baked cookie or two can help win friends and even soften up the opposition.

For nearly a quarter-century, Jordan has been one of the city's best known political operatives — gathering petition signatures to get candidates on the ballot, coordinating local campaigns, raising money and stumping for statewide and national Democrats.

At election time, callers to her home on Brierwood Boulevard even hear a pitch for Democrats on the answering machine.

"Do you want an articulate, progressive and compassionate voice in the U.S. Senate?" was her message several years ago. "Vote for Hillary Clinton in November."

Jordan has also earned a reputation as a highly skilled administrator whose leadership of the Amsterdam and Schenectady municipal housing authorities and success at securing millions in federal grants has been praised by politicians on both sides of the aisle.

Since the day Stratton took office 13 months ago, Jordan has established herself as the second most powerful person in city government.

She reads all of the mayor's mail and consults with him on everything from political appointments to filling potholes and staging press conferences. She manages city employees and puts out small fires that erupt every day.

If somebody calls to complain the garbage wasn't picked up, Jordan makes sure a truck is dispatched to the house.

Her mantra to the staff is simple: No surprises.

"You have to clear things with Sharon," said one person familiar with the inner workings of City Hall.

She also tries to steer coverage of Stratton in the press.

When, on Stratton's first day in office, a reporter learned a secretary was accidentally greeting people on the phone with the former mayor's name, the humorous anecdote never made it into the newspaper. Jordan nixed a secretary's request to let the reporter use the tidbit in a story.

Some chafe under her strict control.

But others say she is a refreshing change from the atmosphere under former Mayor Albert P. Jurczynski, who could take weeks to respond to memos and would hurl profanities when something got under his skin.

"It's very professional," said one department head who has served in both administrations. "She listens to people. I've never seen any bad treatment."

One former administration official described Jordan as an Oz-like figure behind a curtain controlling the mayor's actions. But oth-

Sharon Jordan served as chief of staff
when Brian Stratton was mayor of Schenectady.
[Photo by Marc Schultz, courtesy of *The Daily Gazette*]

ers said the characterization of Jordan as the brains and Stratton as
the pretty face was wrong.

"He tends to deal with the bigger picture and is not immersed
with details, but is very interested in bringing up issues," said Jayme
Lahut, who had a strained relationship with Jurczynski as executive
director of the Schenectady Metroplex Development Authority.
"His own style is refreshing."

As for Jordan, who Stratton appointed to the Metroplex board
of directors, Lahut said, "If she disagrees with what's being said, she
speaks up. She's not a wallflower. But she's very discerning in how
decisions are made. She protects the city's interests but is also accom-
modating and willing to compromise."

Sharon Ann Withrow was born July 23, 1941, in West Lafayette,
Ind., a college town that's home to Purdue University. She was an
only child. Her father, Tommy, owned a small auto sales and parts
business. Her mother, Laura, was a homemaker.

She loved reading as a child and playing at her grandparents'
farm. She said her father was a workaholic and believed in giving
people a second chance.

"That was very important to him and I think it was very informative for me because I believe in that," she said.

Both her parents were Republicans, but that didn't stop her father from being a good friend of the city's mayor, a Democrat. Her own political views came into focus as a student at Purdue after John F. Kennedy was elected president. She admired the young, charismatic Democrat and his policies.

She graduated in 1963 with a double major in elementary education and history. She got a job teaching fourth grade in Racine, Wis. A year later she got married, changing her last name to Jordan.

The couple and their first child, Lisa, moved to Urbana-Champaign, Ill. Jordan was in graduate school when her husband got a job at Knolls Atomic Power Laboratory in 1969. The family settled in Schenectady.

"It was a very nice city, it was great," Jordan recalled. "I loved it. I got involved in politics right away."

She joined a group of reform-minded Democrats and, in 1971, won a seat on the local party committee, a rarity for women at the time. She also gave birth to her second child, Nicole.

In the fall of 1972, she stuffed envelopes and gathered petition signatures for George McGovern, the Democratic presidential candidate. It was around this time that Jordan divorced.

Richard Nixon trounced McGovern in the election, coasting to a victory that proved short-lived when he resigned in 1974 during the Watergate scandal.

Jordan regrouped from the McGovern loss and began working at the Schenectady Community Action Program. In 1975 she became the first female ward president in the city's Democratic Committee, winning the old 11th Ward by a razor-thin margin, 9-7.

"It was difficult, but I've always been able to get along with people," said Jordan, a strong advocate for women's rights. "I think everybody respected me. I was very sincere and really wanted to do the best for everyone."

She worked at SCAP for about eight years, climbing to the No. 2 position before she and the executive director resigned in protest over seniority rules.

She briefly worked as executive director of the New York Conference of Community Action Agencies before taking over as head of the Amsterdam Municipal Housing Authority. Five years later, in 1987, she took over the reins of the Schenectady Municipal Housing Authority.

She retired from the housing authority in January 2003, but emerged a few months later in a familiar role: as campaign manager for Stratton, who was running for mayor.

Stratton, the son of legendary deceased Congressman Samuel S. Stratton, narrowly beat Republican Peter Guidarelli in the race. After the victory, Jordan agreed to serve as the mayor's director of operations on a consulting basis for $25 an hour.

She only expected to help during the transition to power, but neither of them realized the full magnitude of the city's financial crisis and multimillion-dollar deficit.

She ended up staying by Stratton's side the whole year, and has committed to another year at a budgeted salary of $27,500. She works six to seven hours per day, four days a week.

She lives alone and makes a point of going home for lunch every day to let her dog out. On nice days she walks. Otherwise, she hops in her blue PT Cruiser.

Her oldest daughter, Lisa, 40, is a Harvard-educated attorney in Washington, D.C., who works with domestic violence victims. Nicole, 34, lives in Clifton Park. She was an art teacher who decided to switch careers and is about to graduate from massage therapy school.

Jordan's dream came true in September 2003 when Hillary Clinton, now a U.S. Senator, came to a fund-raiser at the Glen Sanders Mansion in Schenectady to endorse Stratton for mayor.

The memory is frozen in time in a framed picture that sits on the corner of Jordan's desk, next to the Senator Schumer cookies.

"I admire her," Jordan said. "She seems to really believe in the issues she talks about. She's so hard working and certainly a role model for women."

*   *   *

Sharon Jordan retired from city hall a few months after Stratton left in 2011, but she remains involved in public service. She's on the board of the Schenectady County Metroplex Development Authority and Schenectady County Public Library, and remains active in Democratic politics.

She was named a Patroon, the city's highest civic honor, in one of Stratton's last acts in office.

When we spoke in October 2018, I asked Jordan about Hillary Clinton's loss in the presidential election. The Schenectady County Democratic Committee had endorsed Clinton for president before she even declared she was running.

"It was absolutely devastating and still is," Jordan said. "I still talk to many of the women who worked with me doing registration and handing out leaflets. Considering the political climate of today is just awful, many times I think about what the country would be like if Hillary had won."

BUYERS
AND
SELLERS

FIGHTING TO TRANSFORM DOWNTOWN ALBANY

August 16, 2013

Albany Business Review

Angelo Maddox has combined hard work and a deep understanding of his customers to find a formula that can work in downtown Albany.

In a city tough on retailers, Maddox owns Fresh & Fly, a store near the Times Union Center that sells merchandise steeped in urban culture.

Hip-hop songs play loudly as customers shop for shirts, pants, shoes, hats, jewelry and handbags in a clean, brightly lit space.

He's competing against suburban malls by selling brands they don't carry, and by staying close to his base. He's also branching out to reach more people without jeopardizing the authenticity his most loyal customers demand.

"I'm in the trenches," said Maddox, 34. "I got my hand on the pulse of urban fashion."

Maddox is showing how an entrepreneur can carve out a niche downtown with the right location, affordable rent and by keeping pace with trends.

A former Golden Gloves boxer, he also has a tenacity borne of a life growing up on the streets of Bed-Stuy, once one of Brooklyn's roughest neighborhoods.

Maddox opened his first store downtown seven years ago, but his entrepreneurial streak goes back to his days at the University at Albany when he sold soaps, oils and lotions during campus events.

"I was an individual who had come from nothing," he said. "I never wanted to be there again."

He has made an impression on many people.

He serves on a retail advisory committee of the Downtown Albany Business Improvement District. In January, during the State of the City speech, Mayor Jerry Jennings said Maddox's ability to overcome personal adversity was inspiring.

He could have easily wound up a statistic, instead of a business owner who is changing the face of downtown.

Maddox spent about $1,000 in savings to open a business called Basic Necessities in July 2006. He sold socks, shoes and other items inside a retail incubator, The Coliseum on Pearl Street, in the city's South End neighborhood.

It took a year or two before the business seemed viable. He expanded, added merchandise and changed the name. He wound up with two stores, one for men and one for women. Even with the growing number of customers, he said there were still people who didn't know where he was located.

He was convinced he could grow the business in a larger, more visible storefront. He found what he thought was the ideal place: a vacant, 1,800-square-foot building at 13 S. Pearl St. that has had a revolving door of food businesses.

The property is owned by The Swyer Cos., whose portfolio includes the upscale Stuyvesant Plaza in Guilderland.

Janet Kaplan, vice president of real estate, remembers being charmed by Maddox on the phone. As a veteran leasing agent, she always has trepidation about mom-and-pop businesses because their enthusiasm usually exceeds their resources.

Angelo Maddox, owner of Fresh & Fly in downtown Albany.
[Photo by Donna Abbott-Vlahos, courtesy of *Albany Business Review*]

She visited Maddox at the Coliseum and liked what she saw.

"He's a nice guy," Kaplan said. "Serious. Bright. He understood the issues he's facing. He's willing to reach out and ask for help."

They both knew he had to diversify the merchandise with business-casual clothes if he moved. That way, he could also appeal to the tens of thousands of office workers downtown.

The new location is just one-third of a mile away from the Coliseum, and on the same street, but might as well be a world apart for some people.

The Coliseum is in the heart of the city's predominantly black South End neighborhood. The building near the Times Union Center is in the central business district downtown.

"The customers I'm getting now wouldn't come to the Coliseum," Maddox said. "Unless they're going to the DMV, that's the only destination."

Maddox was careful not to change so much that he would alienate his core customers.

Many of the brands aren't known to the masses: Kilogram, Rivet De Cru, Fresh Goods and others. There are also household names, such as Ralph Lauren, Levi's and Nautica. A pair of Nike Air Jordans — still fashionable today — costs $174.99.

The clientele is diverse: blacks, Hispanics, white teens, and their parents, from the suburbs.

"The urban culture has broadened into all demographics," Maddox said. "It has no boundaries."

He said the store has done well since he opened there Sept. 20, 2012.

The lease was structured so it would be less expensive up front, while Maddox is building the business. He secured a loan from SEFCU for operating capital.

Maddox has faced a lot of adversity stretching back to his childhood.

His father, also named Angelo, died when he was 4 years old. He was raised by his mother, Shelia, and his paternal grandmother.

When Maddox was getting into trouble in middle school, he moved from Brooklyn to Albany at age 13 to live with his Aunt Betty and Uncle David.

Aunt Betty — Betty Pate — is Maddox's father's sister.

Pate and her husband showed Maddox another way of living. At the time, they were both officers at the Salvation Army on Clinton Avenue.

"We exposed him to attending church and being involved with service work," Pate said. "He began to really see a much broader picture and an area of compassion and giving as opposed to wanting everything given to him."

When he turned 14, he attended a summer youth program that taught him life skills. He also worked as a landscaper and other jobs. Getting paid meant he could buy clothes for school and, he said, "make my own decisions."

"Combined with the atmosphere my aunt and uncle provided for me, the solid family structure, that was an instrumental turning point in my life," he said.

Maddox did well at Philip Livingston Magnet Academy, especially in math, and wrote poetry. Still, he returned to Brooklyn after the summer, and went to a high school in Manhattan.

His aunt had tried to convince him to stay in Albany. But he wanted to reconnect with his mother and friends in the city. She also sensed he wanted freedom from the strict environment in her home.

Maddox fell back in with his old crowd in the city. He didn't go into detail about what happened next, other than to say he was involved in a "violent incident" in Brooklyn at age 16.

"I was charged originally with attempted murder and it got reduced down to self-defense, aggravated assault," he said. "Me and another gentleman had a little disagreement."

He was sentenced to 1-to-3 years in prison. Maddox said he was given youthful offender status, so the records are sealed.

In hindsight, Maddox said, he could have just walked away from the confrontation. He was young, though, and full of bravado.

"You feel like, 'I'm not going to let nobody do anything to me or to hurt me,'" he said.

His family visited him regularly in prison. Their love and support opened his eyes.

He earned his GED in prison, and wrote down a list of golden rules to guide his life. "Keep God first," is at the top.

He moved back in with his aunt and uncle in Albany after getting out of prison in 1999. He went to Hudson Valley Community College, and worked as a youth care counselor, among other things. He also started training at Schott's Boxing in Albany.

Maddox won the 2002 upstate Golden Gloves in the open-class light heavyweight division. He went on to the national competition, but lost his first fight there.

"It was a real accomplishment for him to win a local tournament," said his trainer, Andy Schott, who taught psychology at HVCC.

He remembers Maddox as a quiet, humble and focused student who never missed a class. They had a mutual interest: boxing. Maddox started training at night, eventually sparring.

"The first time I got in the ring, I felt like I was going to die," Maddox said. "He jabbed me to death the whole round. I thought,

'I'm going to get him.' Every day, I just kept coming back and improving my skills."

Maddox got further than many other boxers Schott has trained.

"I did it because I enjoyed it," Maddox said. "My mentality was, wherever it took me, it took me."

After finishing HVCC, Maddox went to UAlbany, where he majored in psychology and minored in business. He graduated in May 2005.

"Once I stopped competing in boxing, I took that same mentality into my business," he said. "I'm not going to lose. I'm going to do whatever it takes to win. You need to do whatever your competitor is not willing to do."

*　*　*

Angelo Maddox continues to own Fresh & Fly in downtown Albany.

In 2018 he was named a "40 Under 40" by the Albany Business Review for his achievements in business.

When asked on the award survey about his proudest accomplishment, he wrote this: "My children! My wife and I have a blended family. We include both our ex-spouses [and their new partners] as a complete part of our family. They are both wonderful people and we're glad that our children have the right village taking care of them. Our children confidently know how much they are extremely loved and cared for by four parents at ALL times. Kids carry themselves differently with that level of confidence and it shows."

ONE NEIGHBORHOOD, TWO DIFFERENT COSTS OF LIVING

January 16, 2005
The Daily Gazette

The Rowell family of Niskayuna and the D'Errico family of Schenectady live close to the same delicatessens, banks, jewelry store and doughnut shop.

If the families knew each other, it would only take five minutes to walk from one front door to the other to borrow a cup of sugar.

But when it comes to the cost of living, the two families in the upper Union Street neighborhood might as well live a thousand miles apart.

They may own similarly assessed houses, but their property taxes and fees put them in two different worlds.

This year, the Rowells, who live in a quaint bungalow at 1282 Dean St. in Niskayuna, will pay $3,544 in town property taxes, school taxes and fees for water, sewer and other municipal services.

The D'Erricos, who live in a slightly larger, classically styled Craftsman at 1265 Baker Ave. in Schenectady, will pay $4,969 in city and school property taxes and fees.

The size of the difference — $1,400 — surprised both families when they were shown an analysis prepared by *The Sunday Gazette*.

"Wow," said Carol Rowell, 46, as she and her husband, Chandler, 52, sat at their dining room table on a recent night.

In Schenectady a few days later, Rick D'Errico and his wife, Betsy, shook their heads in disbelief.

"It is frustrating," said Rick, 37, a reporter at *The Business Review* in Latham. "It's something I knew but it's still frustrating when I see the hard, cold numbers."

The D'Erricos knew taxes were high when they settled in Schenectady nearly four years ago.

But they also knew they could get a bigger house at a lower price than elsewhere, and Rick especially liked the character of old city neighborhoods.

They have grown to love their home, love their neighbors and feel blessed with a great place to raise their two children.

Even so, they say, the streets don't get plowed fast enough in winter; the trash collectors fling their empty garbage cans onto the ground; and the city school district won't bus their kids to their private Christian school in Albany because it's too far away from Schenectady.

Asked whether they're getting what they pay for in taxes and fees, both responded in unison: "No."

The Sunday Gazette asked the Rowells and the D'Erricos to participate in this story after determining both families owned houses in the same neighborhood that are assessed at nearly the same amount, $86,900 and $86,100, respectively.

Property tax bills are based on assessments, not how much a house is worth on the real estate market. Real estate values are markedly different in the city and town.

A house comparable to the Rowells' in Niskayuna sold for $135,000 to $145,000 over the past year.

A house similar to where the D'Erricos live in Schenectady sold for $93,500 to $110,500, according to Doreen Ross, a certified appraiser.

Comparing the costs of living for two families in two different municipalities in the Capital Region is risky because there are so many variables that can make the comparison unfair or inequitable.

One may have municipal water service, the other private wells.

One might be in a growing, financially healthy county; the other in a county struggling with an aging population.

One may have its own police force while the other relies on state troopers and sheriff's deputies to patrol the streets.

Of course, there are significant differences between Schenectady and Niskayuna that go well beyond the way government services are provided.

Niskayuna is one of the wealthiest towns in the region, with a median household income of $70,800, based on the 2000 census, far outpacing Schenectady at $29,378.

The city's population, 61,821, is three times bigger than Niskayuna's.

Schenectady has the worst credit rating in the state and is trying to climb out of a multimillion-dollar budget deficit.

The city is home to major nonprofit institutions, such as colleges, hospitals and county government offices, that don't pay property taxes to offset the cost of providing municipal services.

More than one-third of city property is tax-exempt, compared to 23 percent in Niskayuna.

Schenectady has a full-time paid fire department, while the fire district where the Rowells live relies on a mix of paid and volunteer firefighters and paramedics.

Mayor Brian U. Stratton said Schenectady must pay for a bigger police force than Niskayuna, contend with a shrinking tax base and has more at-risk youth in its schools.

Comparing Schenectady with Albany might be more fair, he said.

"I think inherently it's tough to compare the financial demands of a town to a city," Stratton said.

That said, there are similarities between Schenectady and Niskayuna — both have police departments, provide municipal water and sewer, maintain their own streets and are in Schenectady County.

The upper Union Street neighborhood, located between Union Street and Grand Boulevard, is a good place to compare costs because the town/city boundary cuts diagonally through several streets and the housing stock is very similar on both sides of the line: small bungalows, ranches, Capes and colonials on lots generally measuring one-fifth of an acre or less.

The parallels between the Rowells and D'Erricos are also remarkable: both families have two children and busy, stay-at-home moms; both share a driveway with their next-door neighbor; both are living in the first home they ever bought.

Chandler and Carol Rowell and their two daughters moved to this area from Syracuse after Chandler got a job in the mid-1990s as a research scientist at the New York State Department of Environmental Conservation.

They rented an apartment on Rugby Road in Schenectady for three years before buying a four-bedroom bungalow at 1282 Dean St. in Niskayuna in 1997 for $87,500.

For them, as with many families, the school district was the biggest factor in their decision. Their oldest daughter has Down syndrome, and they were concerned about the level of support she'd receive in the classroom.

They didn't seriously consider buying in Schenectady because they didn't know if Chandler's state job would be permanent. They thought they would have trouble selling a house in the city if they had to move again.

Today the Rowells are very happy with their decision. Their children are doing well in Niskayuna public schools. They don't have any complaints about snow plowing or other town services. They enjoy walking their dog around the neighborhood and participate in an annual block party.

They don't mind only having a one-car garage and a tiny backyard. They don't feel any less safe knowing the town relies on a mix of paid and volunteer firefighters.

Unlike Schenectady residents, they don't have a sidewalk in front of their house, but they can get by without one since their

10- and 12-year-old children have grown older. Streetlights would be nice, though.

"It's a dark block," said Carol, 46, who walks with a flashlight at night for fear she'll get hit by a car.

Rick and Betsy D'Errico were living in Marlboro, Ulster County, when their prayers were answered four years ago: Rick, a daily newspaper reporter, got a job at *The Business Review* in Latham, which meant the couple and their two children could move back to the Albany area and be closer to family.

Friends and relatives warned them not to buy in Schenectady.

But, after looking at 40-some houses in the region, Rick and Betsy found a home in the city that fit their budget and was a short walk to Central Park.

They bought a four-bedroom, 1,890-square-foot Craftsman-style house on Baker Avenue in March 2001 for $93,500. They have a two-car garage and a side yard that makes their property bigger than most city lots.

Other than painting and upgrading some old wiring, the house was in move-in condition. The previous owners had renovated the kitchen.

"I still come down the stairs and say I can't believe it's my house," said Betsy, 35. "It's so beautiful."

Rick's downstate friends were in awe when they saw how much house he was able to buy for less than $100,000.

The low purchase price meant the couple could afford to have Betsy stay home and raise their children. She volunteers a few hours a week at Our Savior's Lutheran School in Albany to save on the kids' private school tuition.

The D'Erricos enrolled their children in a Christian elementary school because they want their faith upheld by teachers in the classroom. Still, it's an extra financial burden on top of a high city property tax and school bill.

"I'm not happy with the taxes," said Rick, 37. "I've talked with Mayor Stratton personally. I don't know how people are going to make it in the city as taxes continue to rise."

*   *   *

This story had an unexpected outcome: it paved the way for me to leave The Daily Gazette for a job at the Albany Business Review.

To research the article I checked property records at the county office building and made a list of addresses that had similar tax assessments on both sides of the municipal border separating Schenectady and Niskayuna. I then tracked down the names and phone numbers of the homeowners and started cold calling.

The challenge was finding two families who would agree to be interviewed. I had never met Rick D'Errico in Schenectady and was surprised to learn he was a reporter at The Business Review [later renamed Albany Business Review]. He and his wife, Betsy, graciously opened their home to me, as did the Rowells in Niskayuna.

After the story was published Rick invited me to lunch. He thought I did a good job and we talked about the news business.

I wasn't looking to leave the Gazette, especially after I was given the coveted state capital beat. But my priorities changed later that year when a position opened up at The Business Review.

By that point I had been a reporter for 13 years. Working late nights, plus holidays and occasional weekends, had grown tiresome. I was no longer a single person living in an apartment. Plus, Lori and I wanted to have children.

A journalism job with a predictable schedule and better pay seemed like the right move. Years later, I know it was the best decision of my career.

LIONHEART PUB OPENS BOOKS ON $3.5 MILLION SALE

April 12, 2015

Albany Business Review

I just saw the last three years of corporate income tax returns for Lionheart Pub, so the $3.5 million sale price — which surprised many people — is easier to understand.

Even so, skeptics may never be satisfied with the explanation.

Jerry Aumand, who sold the tavern and building at 488 Madison Ave. in Albany, showed me the tax returns — along with the signed sales agreement and his personal W-2 for 2013 — providing a rare, inside look at the most surprising business transaction so far this year.

In the few days since *Albany Business Review* broke the story, reaction to the price from the local restaurant, real estate and business brokerage community has been incredulous, to say the least.

How could a small pub near the Center Square neighborhood — an area with 19th-century brownstones, bars and restaurants — possibly be worth that much money?

One real estate broker called it "New York city prices." Another said it was "Cheesecake Factory prices." A third was convinced the $3.5 million figure was a misprint until I assured him it was correct.

With all the doubts and speculation swirling, Aumand approved my request to see the documentation behind the deal. We met Friday morning at his home on a hilltop in North Greenbush to go over the numbers.

Why was he willing to share private information that, frankly, is nobody else's business?

He said the buyer, 39-year-old Mike Keller, a friend who has been in the bar and restaurant business for two decades, has been wrongly portrayed as being taken advantage of in the deal.

"If anything," Aumand said, "Mike should be applauded for something that was thoroughly researched. He was willing to take a big gamble for him, his whole family, and his future. This story is about Lark Street and what Lark Street could offer, not about the businesses that are closed up that couldn't succeed. It's about what you can do when you fight hard and work hard."

I found Aumand engaging, funny and quick with an answer as we sat at the kitchen table of the home he shares with his wife and two dogs. It's a big, welcoming place, with sweeping views of the Albany skyline in the distance.

"This is the house that beer built," Aumand, 58, said with a laugh when we talked about how much his life has changed since the days when he was nearly broke and had to pay the rent at Lionheart with a credit card.

He agreed to show me the financial documents with a few caveats:

I can't reveal his net income during fiscal years 2011, 2012 and 2013.

I can't disclose the exact multiple of the net income that was used to calculate the valuation.

I can't say how the $3.5 million sale price was split between the value of the business and the real estate, but it's public record that a $300,000 mortgage was filed on the property in the Albany County clerk's office.

Jerry Aumand, owner, Lionheart Pub
[Photo by Michael DeMasi, courtesy of *Albany Business Review*]

Aumand is the holder of the note. He also provided financing for the purchase of the business.

Keller and his wife, Julie, made a sizable down payment, based on the March 16 sales agreement.

Here's a number I can share from the tax returns: gross sales at Lionheart Pub in each of the three fiscal years were more than $1 million.

The heart of the matter comes down to a multiple of the net income that determined the pub's value. When you apply that multiple to the net income I saw on the tax returns, and add the cost of the real estate, the math is simple.

Several factors influenced the multiple, Aumand said: a large, loyal customer base; strong profit margins; the financing structure; and the building being included in the sale.

He said a standard multiple range is 5 to 6.5-times net income.

"The multiple that was used was probably a premium," he said, "but a fairly valued premium considering the circumstances."

However, a veteran business broker in Albany not involved in the deal, Kathy Thiel, told me the standard multiple for a bar/restaurant valuation is 1.5 to 3-times discretionary cash flow, which she said can conceivably be the same thing as net income.

Thiel said the range nationally is 2 to 2.5-times, according to The Business Reference Guide, considered the "bible" of business brokerage.

"Frankly a multiple like that [5 to 6.5-times] is for a business that has some kind of specialized service or product," Thiel said. "That to me is a very high multiple for a business like this."

I told Aumand what Thiel said, and he strongly disagreed.

"That's outrageously small," he said. "Maybe it would be that low on leased property. I think they're way off base and don't understand the establishment."

To be fair, Thiel emphasized she doesn't know the details behind the transaction and has never stepped foot inside Lionheart. She was offering up her opinion because I asked for it.

"People ask all the time, what is this worth, what is that worth?" she said. "You really have to know the business. You have to know about the products and customers and how it operates."

An important detail I learned from Aumand is how, when and why Lionheart Pub became so profitable. Conditions were much different in the mid-1990s, when he leased space on Lark Street for what was then a blues cafe with restaurant seating for 34 people.

"It was a very small place, with very high overhead," he said. "I was almost at the point of closing the door. I went five years without drawing a paycheck. Those were very tough times."

The turning point came in 1998-99, when he decided to close the kitchen and focus on selling craft beer. Alcohol has a much bigger profit margin than food because of the high cost of supplies, staffing and waste.

He got permission from the city and state Liquor Authority to switch his business designation from restaurant to tavern, allowing him to serve the bare minimum in food: soups and snacks, such as free popcorn.

He brought in couches, chairs and board games. The size of the English dart leagues eventually tripled. He has beer socials. His regulars include young and old professionals who can order from among three dozen varieties of craft beer on tap. His staff is hard-working and treats customers well.

Aumand moved the business to Madison Avenue, just off Lark Street, after buying a 3,300-square-foot building in 2002 for $175,000. Sales have grown fairly consistently, averaging $1 million or more the past six years, he said.

Keller, the new owner, has room to grow if he chooses. An empty second-floor apartment could be converted into a piano lounge or some other use if he seeks zoning permission and it's granted by the city [Aumand tried twice; he was denied].

Aumand had thought about retiring, but wasn't interested in selling the business until he was approached by Keller a year ago.

Now, he has more free time than he's had since he started running a small design firm in his 20s. He opened Lionheart Pub at age 35.

"It's been very odd and awkward," he said of not working seven days a week, "yet liberating."

* * *

The couple that bought the Lionheart Pub for $3.5 million got in over their heads.

By early 2018 they had fallen behind on their payments to Jerry Aumand, who had provided the loan for the purchase. They owed him more than $3 million and had defaulted on a $300,000 mortgage, according to court papers.

Aumand wound up forgiving the debts in exchange for taking back the business. He was excited about reopening the pub, describing the feeling as "going home again."

HUGH JOHNSON'S CRYSTAL BALL

November 29, 2013

Albany Business Review

A remote-controlled camera is attached to a wall in Hugh Johnson's corner office on the fourth floor of a prominent building in downtown Albany.

Three stage lights are suspended from the ceiling.

Two small strips of orange tape form an 'X' on the carpeted floor.

The ready-to-go TV studio is a hallmark of one of the most recognizable and oft-quoted financial analysts in America, a 73-year-old man with a master's degree in philosophy from Southern Methodist University who became a popular source for business journalists across the world almost by accident.

"It wouldn't have happened, I don't believe, if I hadn't given [someone else] a chance," Johnson said.

The breadth of his media exposure is all the more remarkable since he grew up in Buffalo and has spent most his career working in Albany, 150 miles north of the world's financial capital.

As he prepares for his 25th economic forecast hosted by the Albany-Colonie Regional Chamber of Commerce on Dec. 4, Johnson is thinking about when he will wind down an annual event that typically draws 250 business leaders to hear his insights.

"I know I can't do this forever," he said.

Even if the annual forecasts end at the chamber, Johnson is not considering retiring from Hugh Johnson Advisors, a firm that manages and consults on more than $2.1 billion in assets. He is chairman and chief investment officer.

His health is good. The firm is doing well. And he's still passionate about trying to understand and analyze the direction of the U.S. economy and all the factors that influence it.

As much as CEOs and individual investors rely on him to help decide whether to expand a warehouse or sell their stocks, he's the first to admit he doesn't know what will happen.

"I'm offended when people think they actually know what the future has in store," he said. "They don't, and I don't. I could be wrong, and have been, and I'm not shaken by that."

Humility; a direct way of speaking; and detailed research are some reasons Johnson has become the go-to guy for countless journalists over the past 35 years.

"When I was a young reporter, my editor said go write a story about the stock market," said Will Deener, now a veteran business reporter at the Dallas Morning News. "Hugh never made me feel inferior, no matter how stupid my question was. He always answered in a respectful way. I have learned a lot from him."

Deener, who writes a weekly column about stocks and bonds, said he talks to Johnson at least once a month.

"I have a roster of probably hundreds of analysts and market strategists but I would count him as one of my top two or three favorites," Deener said. "I have gone through many bull and bear markets. I go to him because he's usually right."

Johnson's secretary no longer keeps track of when or where his name appears in stories, but a search by the *Albany Business Review* found he has been quoted in every major news outlet in the U.S. and numerous ones around the world.

Hugh Johnson
[Photo by Donna Abbott-Vlahos, courtesy of *Albany Business Review*]

A few examples are framed on a wall of his office.

One, published Dec. 29, 1989, in a newspaper called Ekonomisk Baksmälia, appears to be written in Dutch or Finnish. Only a few words are in English, including: George Bush, Hugh Johnson, and Charlie Brown of the Peanuts cartoon.

As Johnson tells it, he might not have attracted the attention of reporters were it not for a man named Bill Pundmann.

Johnson was working in the mid-1970s as a director of institutional research at the New York Stock Exchange when a persistent headhunter convinced him to hire Pundmann.

Even though Pundmann had excellent credentials, he had trouble getting a job because he was deaf and had a severe speech impediment. Johnson took a chance on him.

One of the first things Pundmann did was write to *The Wall Street Journal* offering his expertise as an oil industry analyst. A reporter called for an interview, but couldn't understand him.

"*The Wall Street Journal* got off the phone with him and asked me to get on the phone," Johnson said. "They said, 'Sorry, we can't use him, but what do you have to say about the markets?' So I gave them what I had to say. That's the very first time I was quoted in *The Wall Street Journal*. That's where it began."

Johnson left Manhattan in 1977 to work at First Albany Corp., an investment bank and securities brokerage. Its publicist built on Johnson's early media contacts to get him more coverage, raising the firm's stature and bringing in more clients.

The strategy worked so well that in 1988, *The Wall Street Journal* published a story with this headline: "How Market Guru Hugh Johnson Talked His Way to Media Stardom." Naturally, the coverage in the financial world's paper of record raised his profile even higher.

That was in an era before websites and smartphones made Johnson's commentary, and that of any other analyst, instantly available to hundreds of millions of people. Curiously, as the news media's reach has grown faster and wider, Johnson gets fewer calls from reporters these days, typically four or five per week.

He doesn't know why, but guesses the financial press is looking for fresher voices. That doesn't bother him.

He does worry, however, that he hasn't identified someone to eventually take over the job of forecasting financial markets at the firm.

"We certainly have somebody to run the firm in Dan," he said, referring to Daniel Nolan, president and CEO. "He does a great job. That part I'm not worried about, but I do worry about the investment part of our process. I've got my eyes and ears open for anybody that can help us in that respect."

* * *

I typed "Hugh Johnson Advisors" into Google News in September 2018 to see what topics Johnson had recently been called upon by reporters to discuss.

The results included how the economic crisis in Turkey could spark a contagion in global markets [International Busi-

ness Times], his outlook on stocks and investment strategies for oil [Bloomberg P&L podcast] and a decline in U.S. housing starts [National Mortgage News].

I contacted Hugh to ask if he had found someone yet to eventually take over the task of forecasting the financial markets. He said no.

THE
GOOD
LIFE

HOFFMAN'S PLAYLAND ENDS 62-YEAR RUN

September 14, 2014

Albany Business Review

The 62-year run of Hoffman's Playland ended today with hugs, tears, well-wishes, laughter, gratitude, bells ringing, a train whistle blowing and lots of picture-taking as a huge crowd filled the amusement park for the final time in Colonie.

"Thank you so much," Chris Nastke of Valatie said to the park's owners, Dave and Ruth Hoffman, who stood near the front entrance much of the afternoon, in awe of the turnout. "My parents used to bring me when I was little, and I got a chance to bring my little guy today."

It was a sentiment the Hoffmans have heard over and over, especially this season, their last after four decades at the helm. They are retiring and plan to redevelop the roughly 8 acres off Route 9. It's an area that has seen significant change with new stores, restaurants and other businesses nearby.

They also are considering offers to sell the equipment, a deal that would, if finalized, keep the rides in the area, though at a different location.

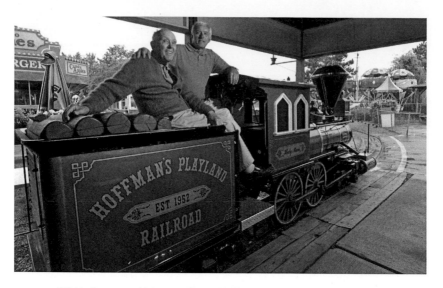

Bill Hoffman and his son, Dave Hoffman, at Hoffman's Playland.
[Photo by Donna Abbott-Vlahos, courtesy of *Albany Business Review*]

The park's final day brought scores of parents, grandparents, children and teens to ride the carousel, bumper cars, paratroopers, Ferris wheel, mini-roller coaster and kiddie train. Most of the prizes in the twenty-five cent arcade were picked clean. Commemorative shirts were selling fast.

Lines were long, especially for the train, but there was a fun, relaxed vibe and a sense people were experiencing the end of an era. Saturday's rain-shortened schedule no doubt added to the size of Sunday's turnout.

The Hoffmans hired three Colonie police officers to monitor traffic and help with crowd control. Although the parking lot was jammed, traffic on Route 9 was moving at a good clip. An officer said there were no accidents or other problems.

The official closing time was 6 p.m. Although most rides for younger children shut down then, a few others were kept going until at least 7 p.m. to accommodate the thinning crowd. The lights were even turned on at the carousel as the sun was setting.

Dave Hoffman said he was asked to pose for a photo hundreds of times. All of the local news media showed up. Hoffman wore a microphone as a crew from Working Pictures trailed him for a documentary being made for local PBS affiliate WMHT-Channel 17.

Hoffman wore dark sunglasses and seemingly perpetual smile.

"It's just been an amazing day," he said.

His 88-year-old father, Bill, who opened the park in 1952 with just three rides, sat on a chair for five hours in the center of the action, enjoying the scene and reminiscing. He said he wasn't sad to see the park close.

"I made a lot of people happy," Bill Hoffman said. "I made my contribution to society."

Joe Abbruzzese, who worked at the park from 1967 to 1971, was thrilled to see his old boss. Bill Hoffman remembered Joe ran the merry-go-round, and was always friendly with people.

"Today, I had to come just to say thank you," said Abbruzzese, owner of Hill Street Cafe on Madison Avenue in downtown Albany.

* * *

Hoffman's Playland closed but the amusement park got a second life at a new location.

The owners of Huck Finn's Warehouse & More in Albany's warehouse district bought most of the rides and moved them to a spot next to their store, rechristening the business as Huck Finn's Playland.

CLOCK FANCIERS SHARE LOVE
OF INTRICATE MECHANICS

May 23, 1999

The Daily Gazette

They call themselves the Monday night clock group. If that sounds a little unusual, well, pull up a chair.

The first order of business for a recent meeting was welcoming a guest, Dave Ashley of Clifton Park. He's built like a football player. He also collects pocket watches. At 32, he's the new kid on the block.

A moment later, just after 7 p.m., Roy Jennings shuffled into the modest hall of the Burnt Hills Baptist Church and took a seat at one of the assembled folding tables.

"Let the record reflect the president is late," cracked Smiley Lumpkin without missing a beat.

Laughter ensued.

Lumpkin, 80, prefers to be called Smiley, and he lives up to his given name with a friendly demeanor and patience for all those unfamiliar with the world of clocks.

Twenty-four men gathered for the weekly meeting, continuing a tradition that began some 15 years ago.

Today many are gray-haired, balding or both, and eyeglasses are the norm. But they have sharp minds — and even sharper wits — and share a love for the mechanical wonders of an old-fashioned clock.

"I always liked clocks," explained Brian Hafler of Ballston Spa who, at 39, represents the new generation of clock hobbyists. "My parents said one of my first words was 'clock.'"

The group's friendly rapport is reminiscent of a 1970s celebrity roast, but updated for the '90s to include a Viagra joke plucked from the internet.

Announcements at the start of the meeting ranged from the rudimentary, like the date of the annual end-of-season dinner, to the personal. One member was in the hospital for a catheterization. Another might need angioplasty.

On this night, Harold Brown brought with him the movement of a pre-1800s-era clock, and perched it atop a wooden pedestal.

The movement is the guts of a mechanical clock — the tidy assortment of notched metal wheels, levers, round plates and pins that rotate and click, making the hands on the face turn.

Smiley Lumpkin with an 1820 Riley Whiting clock built in Winchester, Connecticut. [Photo by Marc Schultz, courtesy of *The Daily Gazette*]

Several men gathered round to catch a glimpse of the movement, admiring it like a newborn baby.

Brown, 73, said his brother-in-law bought the clock at an auction.

Brown tried fixing the antique and was amazed to learn it had no center arbor, a standard feature in most mechanical clocks. A center arbor is the main shaft to which the gears of the minute and hour hands are attached.

"It's an unusual movement," said Brown, who lives in Lenox, Mass., but isn't daunted by the weekly 55-mile drive to the Burnt Hills church.

Three others also come regularly from western Massachusetts. Others hail from Watervliet, Hagaman, Cohoes and Castleton. All told, there are 47 in the group, including two women who show up sporadically.

Members of the Monday night clock group belong to Rip Van Winkle Chapter No. 40 of the National Association of Watch and Clock Collectors, based in Columbia, Pennsylvania.

The Rip Van Winkle chapter draws 80 to 100 people to its bi-monthly meetings in Albany. In the mid-1980s, Lumpkin and a few others decided to start meeting more regularly, and thus was born the Monday night group.

The weekly meetings have continued unabated, except for holidays and during the summer, when they take a break.

Membership is open to anyone interested in clocks. Dues are $40 yearly for the national association, and $7 for the local chapter.

Attendance has grown as word spread. Sometimes, as many as 40 clock hobbyists show up.

"We're getting some young guys, which we're glad to see," said Jack Russell, 72, a neighbor of Lumpkin's in Glenville.

Russell and Lumpkin are the only clock group members who attend Burnt Hills Baptist Church. Close friends, they once worked together at Knolls Atomic Power Laboratory in Niskayuna.

After Lumpkin got Russell interested in clocks, Russell's wife, Anne, bought him a bunch of the specialized tools for Christmas.

"Every time I went to a meeting, she said, 'Don't come home with another clock,'" Russell said wryly. Anne died last September.

On the wall of the church hall is a list of the speakers for each clock group meeting. The duty rotates weekly, and the only requirement is that the presentation has something to do with clocks.

One recent topic was clock nomenclature. For 45 minutes, the men looked at diagrams of clock movements and called out the names of the parts, occasionally disagreeing but never arguing.

The hope was to have a common name for every part, and get away from resorting to "whatchamacallit" and "that thingamajig."

"You don't call that a bushing if there's no bushing there," Brown chimed in when the time came to identify something called a pivot hole.

At 7:25 p.m., a bell tolled once. It was from a clock somebody brought to the meeting and had left sitting on a counter in the corner.

"It works," said Jeff Major, the only club member whose livelihood is repairing clocks.

At the workshop in his Charlton home, Major fixes wall clocks, mantel clocks and cuckoo clocks, and does house calls for grandfather clocks. Appointments are required.

For security reasons, he doesn't publish his address in the phone book or on business cards.

"At any given time I've got tens of thousands of dollars worth of clocks" in the house, Major said.

While many in the group are clock experts, their interest remains just a hobby: collecting, repairing or both.

Several, like Lumpkin, occasionally fix clocks for friends and others. Repairing wristwatches, though, is a specialty that few have learned.

"I enjoy taking a basket case and restoring it to its original workability and beauty," Lumpkin said. "That's probably what I enjoy the most."

In the members' homes, clocks are plentiful. There's a preference for the sound and grace of an old-fashioned clock to the sleekness of today's electronic timepieces.

Still, in the age of VCRs and microwave ovens, it's hard not to have at least one modern clock around.

"I've got a few battery-operated clocks," Russell admitted with a grin. "But I don't tell anybody."

*   *   *

I first heard the name Smiley Lumpkin while seated at the dinner table in the home of my future in-laws, Tom and Fran Mithen.

Somehow we were talking about old clocks, and Tom — now "Dad" to me — said he knew a guy named Smiley Lumpkin who fixes them.

The more I learned about him, the more I realized this could be a fun story to write. How many people named Smiley do you know meet regularly in the fellowship hall of a Baptist church to talk about clocks?

Smiley was a gracious man. His personality lived up to his name. He died July 4, 2010, about a month shy of his 92nd birthday.

"Smiley was a native of Alabama, where he developed a wit and warmth that most of us Yankees can only dream of," his obituary reads. "He was also always the consummate gentleman, and moved with ease among people of different backgrounds. Upon being asked how he came to be named Smiley, he would patiently explain that he was in fact named after his Uncle Smiley. He had a lifelong fondness for telling jokes, many of them requiring exquisite timing and control of intonation and facial expression. He was a great southern humorist in our midst."

OCTOGENARIAN CYCLISTS
TRAVERSE CITY

May 29, 2005

The Daily Gazette

It's hard to miss Floyd and Mary Jane Adamson on the streets of the upper Union Street neighborhood in Schenectady and old Niskayuna.

They ride matching red 21-speed Nishiki bikes. Side-view mirrors are mounted on their black handlebars. L.L. Bean saddlebags straddle the rear wheels.

They pedal at the same snail's pace, about what you would expect from a couple of octogenarian cyclists.

Almost every day for the past 14 years, the Adamsons have pushed the bikes out of the single-car garage at their Sumner Avenue home and gone for a spin. Their usual route is about 10 miles.

Floyd is 86; Mary Jane, 80.

It's clear they don't act their age.

"You can not feel too well, and get some exercise, and you feel a hell of a lot better," Floyd said, summing up the psychology behind the married couple's devotion to their daily trips around town.

A next-door neighbor, William Hubbard, a retired insurance executive, vouches for their longevity. He's about the same age, and laughed when asked whether he and his wife, Charlotte, ever join the Adamsons.

"Never," he said. "We don't ride. I haven't ridden bikes in years. I'm absolutely amazed, because at their age I would not expect them to be as diligent as they are. They're delightful people. This is something they've done together since the time they met."

In fact, bicycle riding is how they met.

It was October 1990. Floyd and Mary Jane were both widowed. He lived in Baltimore. She was in Schenectady. They each signed up for a stay at an elder hostel in the Catskills that included a weeklong, 400-mile bicycle ride.

Biking had been a passion of Mary Jane's since her teenage years. For Floyd, a retired Westinghouse electrical engineer with too much time on his hands, it was an activity one of his sons had suggested he take up just six months earlier as a way to keep busy.

By the end of the trip through the Catskills, they had exchanged phone numbers.

Before she knew it, Mary Jane was driving to Baltimore with her bike in the trunk to visit Floyd. They rode around Gettysburg and other parts of southern Pennsylvania.

Five months later, on March 23, 1991, they got married and moved to Mary Jane's house in Schenectady. It was her third marriage and his second.

Initially, their rides were more for exercise and convenience than out of habit. They would burn calories instead of fossil fuels to get to the bank or store down the block. They participated in a regional bicycling club's century ride, a 114-mile trek that Floyd says "pretty near-well killed me." [The route was only supposed to be 100 miles, but they got lost.]

They also ventured overseas, going on excursions in Spain, England, Germany, Denmark, France, Austria and the Netherlands. Their days of staying at elder hostels wound down, however, when they real-

Mary Jane and Floyd Adamson prepare for a bike ride.
[Photo by Meredith L. Kaiser, courtesy of *The Daily Gazette*]

ized the rides were turning into competitions. It's hard to keep up with somebody 25 years younger who's also considered a "senior."

"They're too fast for me anymore," Floyd said.

The couple uses an odometer to keep track of the miles they log every year, and Floyd dutifully changes the battery each Jan. 1. Mary Jane has the numbers written down on small strips of paper: 1997 - 1,650 miles each; 1998 - 2,140; 2001 - 2,350; 2002 - 1,950; 2003 - 1,600; 2004 - 2,300.

As of a couple weeks ago, they had racked up 654 miles so far this year. Average speed was 8.5 mph.

Word to the wise: Remove hearing aids before going for a spin, or else it's just too noisy.

Despite all those miles on all those roads, they have only been in a couple of crashes. Floyd's bike was stolen once while parked outside of a Price Chopper. Another time, the seat was swiped while outside the Schaffer Heights senior citizen apartments.

Naturally, so much riding has helped keep them healthy, though they feel the aches and pains of old age. Mary Jane is rail thin, weighing the same today as when she was 18 years old. She says she can still fit into the wedding dress she wore for her first marriage.

"It's probably in the genes," said Mary Jane, who comes from a family of hikers.

They have eased back on their winter rides, no longer venturing out unless it's at least 40 degrees and not icy [their threshold used to be 20 degrees]. They have a stationary bike and a treadmill, but Floyd described them as "very boring."

On good-weather days, when his body tells him no, Floyd listens to the other voice in his head — and the voice of the person in the room with him — telling him yes.

"I decide I'll feel better if I do it," he said.

*   *   *

Mary Jane Adamson died January 20, 2011.

She was survived by five children, seven grandchildren, two great-grandchildren, six stepchildren and a number of step-grandchildren.

I learned from her obituary she was the high school vale-dictorian in her hometown of Phelps, New York, a village in Ontario County. She was just 19 years old when she graduated from William Smith College in 1944 with a bachelor's degree in science.

"She loved to bicycle, swim, play bridge with dear friends, tend a garden, and hike into Lake Saint John in the Adirondack Mountains," her obituary reads. "Being a talented seamstress, she sewed nearly all of her clothes."

RED SOX FANS
REGISTER PRIDE WITH DMV

December 30, 2004
The Daily Gazette

After 86YRS the 04BOSOX finally won the World Series, meaning the dreaded Curse of the Bambino has at long last been REVRSD.

If it still hasn't sunk in for Yankees fans, just take a closer look at the New York state license plate on the car that might have passed you on the road today.

As they would say in Boston, ITZOVA.

Boston Red Sox fans across the Empire State have let their true colors show since their team swept the St. Louis Cardinals 4-0 in late October. The Sox clinched their first World Series crown since 1918.

In the first month after the team's historic Oct. 27 victory, 99 vehicle owners in New York registered new vanity plates bearing a message about their beloved Sox, according to a list compiled by the state Department of Motor Vehicles.

Nine others got a standard plate with the Red Sox team logo.

There's a FENWAY [a tribute to the team's ancient ball park in Boston], a BYENYY [rubbing it in the faces of Yankees fans, no doubt] and CHMP04 [isn't that one obvious?]

There's also kudos to individual players: MANEE [slugger Manny Ramirez], JASVK [catcher and team leader Jason Varitek] and PAPI34 [clutch home run hitter David Ortiz].

Don't be fooled into thinking the state is awash in Red Sox red.

At last count, there were slightly more than 10,000 license plates devoted to the clean-cut Yankees, compared with just 356 for that scrappy, long-haired team from New England.

Schenectady County Public Defender Mark Caruso, a native of Waltham, Massachusetts, and lifelong Sox fan, saw a vanity plate a couple years ago at the mall honoring pitching ace Pedro Martinez.

"I saw that and said if they ever win, I'll get one," said Caruso, 37.

Sure enough, after the Sox won the Series — Game 4 happened to fall on Caruso's birthday — he paid $68 for a plate with a Red Sox logo that reads REVRSD.

In Red Sox lore, the team had been cursed ever since it traded Babe Ruth to the Yankees after winning its last World Series in 1918. Reversing the Curse became the dream of legions of fans.

Friday is the last day drivers in New York can get new "picture plates" with an out-of-state baseball team's logo because the licensing agreement with Major League Baseball is expiring, according to DMV spokesman Joe Picchi.

Personalized New York state license plates will continue to be available after Friday, but not with the Red Sox logo or any other out-of-state baseball team. Those plates cost $50 on top of registration fees.

Denise Baker, of Schenectady, who works as a nurse at Glendale Nursing Home, got BYBABE on her 1995 Jeep Wrangler. It's the latest salvo in her intense but friendly rivalry with her neighbor on Olean Street, Charlie Hebert, who loves the Yankees.

"I just wanted to get 'em so I could get him good," the 50-year-old Baker said.

Denise Baker of Schenectady with her Boston Red Sox vanity license plate.
[Photo by Hans Pennink, courtesy of *The Daily Gazette*]

Randy Tyx, a metal industry sales representative who lives in a suburb of Buffalo, suffered for years as a fan of the Red Sox, football's Buffalo Bills and hockey's Buffalo Sabres — teams that have crushed their fans' hearts year after year.

"I was oh-for-my-life until this," said Tyx, 48. "I have three boys who are Red Sox fans, too. Every year I would apologize to them."

His oldest, 22-year-old Jason, is a weather forecaster for the Marine Corps stationed at Camp Fallujah in Iraq. During the World Series, Jason woke up at 3 a.m. to watch the games on TV and would e-mail his father every night to chat about what happened.

Tyx drives a company car, so the vanity license plate he chose ended up on his wife's 2003 Chevy Cavalier, which just happens to be painted in what he called "Red Sox red."

After toying with a few names on the DMV web site they came up with ITZOVA, a play on a true Bostonian's pronunciation of "It's over."

"We get a lot of compliments on it," said Tyx, who is thinking about making his first-ever drive to Boston in the car to see his team play at Fenway Park.

That is, if he can score tickets for next season.

*   *   *

The Red Sox won three more World Series after that incredible 2004 season, including in 2018 when they beat the Los Angeles Dodgers just as this book was going to press. I never got a vanity license plate, but I still hate the Yankees.

TEN
MINUTES
WITH

DAWNMARIE A. VANN

Owner, A-1 R.E.O. Services LLC

DawnMarie Vann, owner of foreclosure specialist A-1 R.E.O., doesn't hold back when it comes to sharing stories about her life and business. Buckle up and get ready for an adventure.

You had an interesting upbringing as one of 11 children.

My parents were originally from Massachusetts. They were next-door neighbors in a duplex. They became lovers. They were both married to someone else at the time. My mother got pregnant. My mother already had a son and my father had five children when they took off together. My father packed them up and they moved to California. They thought they would strike it rich, but that didn't work out. They ended up coming here and by now they were divorced [from their first spouses]. They didn't find out until years later their divorce wasn't legal.

What did they do?

When they found out their marriage wasn't legal, they went and got married. They loved each other very much.

Did your parents' past bother you?

I didn't learn until I was 15 that I had half-sisters and half-brothers. I found out at a cousin's wedding, where my dad gave away the bride. I didn't understand why my dad was doing that. At the end, I was with one of my cousins who was saying goodbye. She said, 'Goodbye, Dad.' That's when I learned my 'cousin' was actually my half-sister. My family is so dysfunctional, but at least we put the fun in dysfunctional.

How big is your family?

My father was the oldest of 14. I have 44 first cousins.

You started selling real estate in the mid-1980s but stopped a few years later. Why?

My father died in 1989. He owned a business in Guilderland, Audio-Visual Sales & Service. He sold to hospitals, schools, prisons. I left real estate to incorporate his business, get it modernized. I registered it as a woman-owned business for my mom.

After that you and your husband Bob started a business called QVZ Sales. What was that?

I was an itinerant merchant. I was like a Gypsy. We bought a 15-passenger van and traveled around the country selling costume jewelry. I would book a 5,000-square-foot room in a hotel. My husband would buy the inventory and do the ads on radio and TV. We did about $10,000 a day. In Tuscaloosa, Alabama, we did $23,000 in one day. Selling junk.

Tell me about your sale in New Orleans.

We had 18-wheeler trucks parked inside the Superdome. They looked tiny. The sale was in a building next to the dome. On the first day of the sale people were lined up to get in.

DawnMarie A. Vann, owner A-1 R.E.O. Services
[Photo by Michael DeMasi, courtesy of *Albany Business Review*]

How did the sale go?

We did $205,000 that one day. We'd have these drop safes and armed security. I had to go to the bank three times in a limo with the cops because the money was coming in so quick.

Why did you wind down the business in the mid-'90s?

There was saturation in the market. Plus I got sick and tired of eating in restaurants. We traveled 300 nights out of the year. I went back to working at Re/Max and helped an agent named Cathy Patten who was sick at the time. Most of her business was foreclosures.

What did you learn about the foreclosure business?

Back then you were given a form with the information about the house. It had been photocopied so many times it was hard to read. You had to glue a picture of the house onto the paper. I bought a laptop and software called OmniForm. I could create camera-ready ads, reproduce the forms and make it look pristine.

What happened then?

Some of the bank clients asked me to send them my forms. I realized I could streamline the business. After working for Cathy for six months I thought I'd prefer to be her competitor. I went to Prudential Manor Homes and said they needed an R.E.O. (real estate-owned) specialist. They agreed to take me on.

Why did you only stay 18 months?

I was doing $2 million a year in sales, and thought I could do more. But I needed assistants. I started A-1 [in 2000] and every year it got better and better. It went from $2 million to 6 to 8 to 10 to 12 to $15 million, but then it went back to $12 million. At this point, it might get back to $10 million.

What's the toughest part of the business?

Cash flow. It's costing me about $3,000 per asset to get homes ready. Cleaning out the trash, winterizing them, snow removal. I could spend $2,000 a week alone on snow removal. The reimbursements from the banks can take 30 to 120 days.

Some would say you profit from other people's misery by specializing in foreclosed homes. What do you say?

I look at it totally differently. You want to borrow money from me. I'll loan it to you. I expect you to pay me back. You don't pay me back, and you're miserable? What about me?

Do you have any sympathy for people in foreclosure?

Oh, of course I do. I'm not heartless. I can't tell you how many people have come into my house because they have nowhere else to go. I call it Bob's bed-and-breakfast.

How is Bob's health?

He had to be hospitalized in 2002 for kidney failure. He became so disabled he had to be unemployed. He's on dialysis. I realized I had to take this business a whole lot more seriously. I had to make more income to plan for our retirement.

You started taking time for yourself to relieve stress. Was that hard to do?

It was real difficult. I didn't realize it but I was living like solitary confinement. I didn't go out. I didn't socialize with friends because I had a sick husband.

Where do you go?

A couple of years ago a girlfriend invited me to the Honda Classic, a PGA tournament in Florida. That changed my life. I took up golf. I joined a country club. I bought Ping golf clubs. I joined a gym. I got back into good shape. I fly down once a month for a getaway of shopping and golfing. We go out and dance the night away.

December 3, 2010
Albany Business Review

*   *   *

Bob Vann died Nov. 20, 2011 from end stage renal disease. He was 61.

I contacted Dawn over the summer of 2018 to let her know I was publishing this book and asked if I could take her picture because the one we had on file needed updating. I also wanted to interview her for a story I was working on about the sale of foreclosed homes. It had been many years since we last spoke but without hesitation she said yes.

When we met we talked about Bob's death; her grandchildren; and the big tree that had fallen in her backyard after a recent storm, just barely missing the swimming pool.

She's still listing foreclosed homes, but the volume has dropped considerably since the 2007-09 recession ended. Her inventory has been cut in half.

I asked if anyone should feel bad for her.

"Absolutely not," she said. "Like any real estate business, we have our highs and our lows. I expect in a couple of years we'll see it begin to turn again."

Ten Minutes With — 189

KIMBERLY ADAMS RUSSELL

President, Frank Adams Jewelers

The word driven can be defined as 'motivated or determined by a specified factor or feeling.' Here's another way of putting it: 'Kimberly Adams Russell.'

You were diagnosed with Multiple Sclerosis six years ago. How did that come about?

Stress. I was seriously a workaholic — 12-, 15-, 18-hour days, seven days a week. We had three children [including twin girls]. It was hard. I literally called in payroll on a Thursday, had a C-section, and paid my staff the following Thursday. I never missed a beat. When the babies were little, they never slept. At the time, we were renovating this store. We had construction problems. When the construction phase really hit a wall, I woke up one morning and I couldn't get out of bed. I was numb everywhere. I thought I had a stroke. By the end of the day I knew I had MS.

What was your reaction when the doctor told you?

Frankly, in a strange sort of way, I was relieved. It's not life threatening. I was almost grateful, which sounds kind of weird. I had a really good support system. My family was wonderful. Once I knew what I had, I could deal with it.

Kimberly Adams Russell, president, Frank Adams Jewelers
[Photo by Donna Abbott-Vlahos, courtesy of *Albany Business Review*]

Did the diagnosis change how driven you are?

You're never going to change the fact you're driven, but I did re-evaluate a lot of my life at the time. I was really not exercising. I wasn't eating that well. I'm in better health today than I was then. Eating all natural foods, paying more attention to what you put in your body.

I'm told that if you took a real vacation you would feel on edge.

I would. I'm not good at vacationing.

What is the most relaxing thing you've done lately?

I got a massage in New York a couple nights ago.

Was that a special treat or do you make a point of doing that?

I make a point of it, but I do it more for my health than for relaxation.

How do you de-compress?

I'm not good at that. I don't need a lot to de-compress. I don't carry stress really heavily. At that time I did, but day-to-day stress I can actually roll with the punches pretty well.

Do you like to hang out at home on Sundays in your worst sweat pants?

Yeah, I need one day home. I have to say that's one thing I love about winter, because I want to make a big fire. When we built our house I wanted a real fireplace, not a gas fireplace. I had to have real wood. And I want to make sauce, have some wine with my friends. Almost every Sunday we do family day at home. I need a lazy day home with my kids.

You graduated from Ithaca College in 1991 with a degree in speech communication. Did you know what kind of job you wanted to pursue?

No, I thought I would go into college admissions. I did explore broadcast journalism. My dad asked me to help him come up with a new marketing campaign. I taught classes with the Knowledge Network. I was really into the community at that time. I was single. What else was I doing?

What are your earliest memories of your grandfather's jewelry store in downtown Albany?

I don't have a lot of recollections of my grandfather personally. I remember him in our house playing with us as kids, but not as a businessperson.

Was there an expectation you would work at the jewelry store?

No, they never pressured me at all. I think they probably hoped — because if they thought of the three siblings, I would be the one that's the best fit — but they never pressured me at all. I just wanted to help. We were in downtown Albany. It was a very well run, kind of enchanting little store. Very old school. I wanted to make it fresher. I felt like we needed to create more women clientele and a younger audience.

Did you come up with slogan, 'Where the Name on the Box Means Excitement'?

That was my grandfather's. That predated me. I was cleaning the store, going through all these old files, old articles we had, and old ads. We had been in that location for so long, nobody threw anything out. I found that slogan among all the things he had done. It had probably not been used since the '60s or '70s.

Men dominate the jewelry industry. Has it been difficult for you to feel accepted?

I think it was when I was younger. Honestly speaking, in my industry I have never really been in a position where I felt I wasn't held in high regard.

What about outside the jewelry business?

Even though I'm president of the company, people still call me all the time and ask for my husband to make financial decisions. Or my dad. I'm a 41-year-old person. I can make those decisions by myself. But I still do get that. Many women I'm sure do.

Can you spot fake jewelry a mile away?

Yeah, but that's OK. I think a lot of women can wear costume jewelry and fine jewelry and mix it together and still create a fabulous look.

May 4, 2009
Albany Business Review

*   *   *

Even though we graduated from the same college in the same year, I didn't know Kimberly Adams Russell until I started working at the Albany Business Review.

I've interviewed her several times over the years, but we hadn't spoken in a while when I contacted her in September 2018 to get an update on her personal and professional life.

She had a second jewelry store in Saratoga Springs but closed it to focus on the flagship store at Stuyvesant Plaza in Guilderland. She said it was one of the smartest decisions she has made "for my lifestyle, overall health and the success of my business."

"I was able to truly focus on the growth of my business and be a strong leader for my staff," she wrote in an email. "Since that time I have remodeled the store adding a Rolex boutique and an authorized Rolex service center. Frank Adams is currently one of only four official Rolex jewelers to have an in-house approved repair center."

The change enabled her to spend more time with her family. Her twin daughters are 16-years-old; her 21-year-old son is getting an MBA at Quinnipiac University. He intends to go into the family business, becoming the fourth generation to do so.

As for her Multiple Sclerosis, she has been able to manage the disease by limiting stress.

"I try to get as much sleep as I can since fatigue is one of my symptoms," she wrote. "My family and staff are very supportive of me."

ROCKY COCCA

Owner/managing partner, Cocca's Hotels

Rocky Cocca had a tough upbringing. But those years taught him the value of hard work and living within his means. Good lessons for an owner of six hotels.

You were 5-years-old when your mother, Rachel, died of cancer. That must have been difficult.

She was sick for a couple of years so we really didn't know her that well. She had two other boys that were 10 and 12 from another marriage. They probably suffered a lot more than [my brother] Jimmy and I. She was a remarkable woman from what we know of her.

Your father, Frank Sr., owned a diner in Watervliet and some local hotels. He was also a bookie.

He was a good bookie, an honest bookie. *The Times Union* did a major story on him. He served time in jail. Twice. Three months at 70 years old, and a year in 1960.

How did that affect you?

Well, my mother passed away at the time he was in jail. It was kind of weird. We were living with our uncle. We didn't know where my father was. They told us he was in college. That's where we thought he was at that age. We were told years later.

Did he have to raise you on his own?

He remarried and we didn't get along with his third wife. Ultimately we were brought up through the hotels. He bought his hotel on the corner of Wolf Road and Central Avenue in 1967. I was 12 years old when I started living there.

How long did you live at the hotel?

We kind of got moved around. At 11 or 12 years old, I [moved there] until I was 14. At 14 I went to live with my father's first wife in Watervliet. She said she would take me. I didn't want to go. I liked living alone. It was fun. She took me in, registered me for school. I lived there for three months and it was an interesting experience because it was one of the few times I woke up in the morning and had a closet with clean clothes.

Who took care of you at the hotel?

It was staffed 24 hours. Dad would pick us up and bring us to school. Our babysitters were the front desk people.

In hindsight do you feel part of your childhood was lost?

Well, we had a pretty good childhood. We were pretty much free to do whatever we wanted, but he made us know the value of a dollar. When we wanted money he made us work for it. We didn't mind working for the money because we had cash and could go out and spend it with our friends and go out and terrorize Colonie Center.

Did you work at the diner in Watervliet?

It was a 24-hour diner. The place was hopping all the time. One of the reasons I got into the hotel business was because at 18 I used to cook midnights for him flipping eggs. At 3, 4 o'clock in the morning these people were coming from everywhere. As the customers are coming in I'm getting aggravated. It's hot in the kitchen. He's out

Rocky Cocca, owner/managing partner, Cocca's Hotels
[Photo by Donna Abbott-Vlahos, courtesy of *Albany Business Review*]

there taking cash at the register. There's lines. I said if you can't be happy when you're busy it's not the right business to be in.

What's different about the hotel business?

You work hard getting busy, filling the house, and when the house is full, it's fun. You meet the guests in the morning, socialize a little bit, learn a little about them.

You and your brother, Jimmy, who runs one of the six Cocca hotels, learned street smarts.

Jimmy and I aren't highly educated. We were rats. My father was a great father and a good provider but that was it. Here's $5, go get something to eat. He was busy with his business, whether it was booking or the hotels.

I think your brother used the term "stray cats."

Stray cats. What did I say, rats? Yeah, we were stray cats, exactly, but we were good kids.

Did you have fun?

For us at the time it was. Looking back, it could be almost trouble today. I can't imagine raising a 12-year-old daughter or son and having them sleep in a hotel by themselves. Those times were different. We were city kids. We would go anywhere on our bikes. Hitchhiking was OK. You weren't afraid to do anything and my father kept a good eye on us.

What lessons did you learn from your dad?

Never spend more than you make. Never live beyond your means. Always have a slush fund around. Those little things make sense. You can't get away with spending more than you make for a long time, but times change. You have to make investments. Things right now aren't good for the hotel industry, but we don't want to look at it as not being good. We want to survive and look for opportunities. We know there's going to be a lot of hotels failing in the next year. Maybe there's another opportunity. We're not over-leveraged, so we'll be fine.

You recently acquired your sixth hotel, the former Econolodge off Wolf Road.

We have 370 rooms, doing almost $4.5 million a year. We have to learn how to manage the managers now. We listen to our guests and our employees. If we could be at every location every time we know we'd have success.

What's the hardest part about owning hotels?

We always want to give customer satisfaction, but I think it's keeping your staff and teams motivated and comfortable. We're not paying high salaries to a lot of our employees. We employ about 80 people, most of them are $8 to $10 an hour employees. We're mom and pop — we're behind the desk. You'll never see me in a shirt without the Cocca's logo on it unless I'm wearing a shirt and tie and I'm out to dinner. We're always trying to promote our brand.

August 17, 2009
Albany Business Review

*   *   *

Rocky Cocca is still in the hotel business but he now owns just two properties, both on Wolf Road in Colonie.

The others were sold as part of an ownership transition in his family.

When we spoke in September 2018 he was in the midst of buying out his brother's stake in the remaining two hotels. Jimmy Cocca had remarried and moved to Myrtle Beach to manage his daughter's cupcake bakery, Coccadotts.

"With his lifestyle and his move we decided the partnership is not the way to go," Rocky said. "If you're not willing to invest in the long term you have to get out."

Once the deal with his brother is finalized Rocky intends to upgrade both locations. He's tired of explaining to guests why their $49-a-night room doesn't come with a free breakfast.

"I am hungry to get out of the economy business," said Rocky, who is 63. "I have a passion for the hotel business, but I don't want to operate them. I want to develop them and bring in a management company to run them."

MICHELE RIGGI

President, National Museum of Dance

About her home: Built in 2003 at a cost of more than $6 million, the nearly 20,000-square-foot mansion on North Broadway — called "Palazzo Riggi" — has six bedrooms, 10 bathrooms, a bowling alley, fitness center and an outdoor dog run with heated pavers.

About the family fortune: Ron Riggi is CEO, owner and co-founder, with his twin brother, Vincent, of Turbine Services Ltd., which supplies non-Original Equipment Manufacturer replacement parts for General Electric Co.'s heavy-duty gas turbines. The company is headquartered in Saratoga Springs.

The summer party season is about to get even hotter in Saratoga Springs, and Michele Riggi will be in the middle of it all — attending fundraisers, kissing cheeks at soirées, wearing fashionable hats at the track. She's a celebrity socialite, and heir-apparent to Marylou Whitney, the reigning queen of Saratoga high society. She's also a lightning rod for criticism because of her extravagant home and luxurious lifestyle she shares with her husband, Ron. Michele makes no apologies for her favorite things, loves helping the less fortunate, and doesn't shirk life's unglamorous duties. She's a philanthropist who picks up her dogs' poop.

The shelves of your office are filled with white plastic binders. What's the story?

That's my life. Everything I do is categorized.

Why?

Because I have to be organized. I'm like a neat nut. I can't be successful if I'm not organized. At any one time if somebody calls me and wants to know something that I did last year, I need to be able to pull the binder out and go to the tab and say, 'OK, this is the bill. This is what we're aiming for this year.'

How many fundraising events do you attend every year?

Over 100.

What types of events?

We are really huge into the arts. I'm the president of the National Museum of Dance. That is like a day-to-day job for me. I have a gala every night.

Do you ever get tired of attending these events?

No. The reason why we don't tire is my husband loves to go out every night. We'll go to the fundraiser, and then we go out together. It's not like we stay at the events all night. We make an appearance and then we go. That way, it's not draining on us.

Do you actually eat at the events?

I never eat at the events.

Why?

I don't do buffets.

Why?

I don't like people touching the food and then, like, putting it back. Breathing over it, like if they're sick. I skeeve that. That's some-

Michele Riggi, president, National Museum of Dance
[Photo by Donna Abbott-Vlahos, courtesy of *Albany Business Review*]

thing I just never do. We always have a cocktail and then we go out to dinner after, but never, ever, eat at an event. And breath, I can't stand the breath. If somebody eats a crab cake and then starts talking to me, I want to throw up. I'm like, oh God, breath is disgusting. It's bad enough normal breath for people, but when you start eating and you have things in your teeth, it's so annoying. It's so rude.

You must encounter this a lot.

I do.

If you see somebody with a little piece of lettuce in their teeth will you tell them?

Yes, or something hanging out of their nose, of course. I wish people would tell me that. 'Your hair is messed,' and I know it so can you just fix that little hair that is hanging out.

What is your favorite organization to support?

The National Museum of Dance because I was a dancer.

What kind of dance did you do?

Everything. I started dancing when I was 5. My mother was a dance instructor. I danced my whole life, and I'm still dancing.

What kind?

I work out two hours a day so my Pilates is kind of like my dance. I do handstands in my workouts, and I do cartwheels. I do all kinds of stuff to keep agile.

Do you have a personal trainer?

I have three trainers.

Three? Why do you need three trainers?

[To] look like this. I have a Pilates trainer four days a week. I have a boxing trainer once a week. I can hit that speed bag like no other, and then I do my core with him and my cardio. And I have a weight trainer three days a week because you have to have muscles, too.

Summer is the peak season for events. Do you get burned out?

No, I really enjoy it. My feet get tired. I wear my stilettos.

What's your secret for maintaining stamina?

You need to get your sleep. I try to get in bed every night before 11 and I sleep until 7:30 or 8 o'clock. I really need my sleep. I never sit down during the day unless I'm driving. I'm standing all day long working and then at night my husband will get home and he's like, 'You're not in the shower yet.' I'm like, 'I'm just finishing up.' Then we go to the events.

How many pairs of shoes do you own?

Hundreds.

Your favorite designer?

Christian Louboutin.

What's your annual clothes budget?

I don't have a budget.

How much do you spend on clothes?

You should ask my husband that question. I don't even know.

On Halloween, you dress as Cinderella and hand out candy bars at your home.

I love it. The kids go crazy.

Is there a line up the block?

5,000 people come through the gates. I get my picture taken with every one of them. This year we gave out 10 or 12 golden bars with a $100 bill in them.

What does Michele Riggi do to let her hair down?

I love going to our home in Lake Placid. I put my jeans on, my cowboy boots and my hat, and off we go with the dogs. The other night we were at a Toby Keith concert. I take a girl day and we go party all day. Believe me, I know how to enjoy myself.

How many dogs do you own?

Forty dogs, and one cat, Emerald.

That poor cat.

No, she's such a queen. We just rescued her [in November].

What made you get a cat?

I was at the hospital down in Latham with two of the dogs getting their hearts checked. She was in a crate in the waiting room and I've been wanting a cat and my family keeps telling me you're not going to get a cat. I'm like, first of all, you can't tell me what to do. I will do what I want. The more they said no you can't have a cat, the more I wanted one. It took about a year and I knew he or she would come to me.

Will people be surprised to know you got a cat?

Everybody who knows me knows it. I have like 4,000 Facebook friends, and she's on my Facebook like once a week. We send out 1,000 Christmas cards and she was on the Christmas card this year.

How much do you spend on dog food?

How about asking how much I spend on grooming every four weeks, because I just hate it. I'm just, like, I think I should start grooming my own dogs. It's like $2,500.

What kind of food are they fed?

We cook for the dogs. We buy 200 pounds of meat every four weeks, 100 pounds of organic chicken, 100 pounds of 90-percent-lean ground beef. You just have to imagine the refrigerator when that comes.

How is it prepared?

We boil the chicken. Once it's cooked, we take the breasts out and cool them, and then that whole big stockpot is chicken soup. Then the breasts get put into a food processor and we make it into almost like hamburger. Then we freeze four cups at a time in a Ziploc bag and make them flat. Then the beef gets sautéed. We throw out the fat, and the same thing happens [as with the chicken]. Every day, we take one of those Ziplocs out and mix it with four cups of Wendy Volhard's Foundation Diet, which is an oats and grains mixture. It's like oatmeal. That goes together with the protein, plus eight cups of warm water and you mix it up. It's like a soupy goulash, like chili consistency. They get fed fresh a half-cup or a third-cup, whatever the size dog. It's all individual.

Are you doing this yourself or do you have assistants?

In the mornings, my husband feeds 28 dogs upstairs. I used to do it but he took it away from me because he doesn't really spend a lot of time with them like I do. So he likes to interact with them. He feels that's the time in the morning before he goes into work when he can relax. While he's doing that, I am mopping, picking up poop, throwing the wee-wee pads in the garbage, putting the poopy down the toilet. That's where the poopy goes. I have two dogs in wheelchairs, so those guys get special attention. Usually I have to give them a bath once a day. People don't realize we are hands-on with our animals.

You were in talks with Ryan Seacrest Productions about a reality TV show based on your family's life. It would have aired on the E! cable channel. Why didn't that come together?

They didn't pick us up because we didn't have enough drama in our family.

Why were you interested in doing the show?

Because we have a fabulous family. We have a really unique family. We have great kids. We live with 40 dogs, 18 koi fish, 19 canaries, 15 saltwater fish, a cat. All of our children are very successful, and I wanted to show the world that there are people out there — not that we are like the "Leave it to Beavers" or "Brady Bunch" — but there's so much bad stuff on TV right now in the reality realm. Kids are growing up with such bad role models and we're really good people. I wanted the country to see there were good families. I mean, we have drama every day here, but they wanted dirty drama and that's not what I wanted.

Will there be another opportunity?

You never know. Maybe in the future there might be a show about me instead of the family. I don't know. I would be up for that. There's so much for me to share with the world, with the country, and animals, and what we do.

I have to ask a difficult question. How much does it bother you to know there are people out there that don't like the lifestyle you live? They think that it's ostentatious, that it's superficial, and it's ridiculous to have 40 dogs?

Those dogs, probably 20 of them, are rescues. I don't think people realize that. Most of the dogs people actually dropped off here or that I rescued from bad situations. I have dogs that are deaf, blind, that have no teeth, no voice. We have a lot of dogs that are really problem dogs. I would never turn my back on anyone who needs a home for a dog. It doesn't bother me that people don't like me because people don't know me. When they do get to know me, they like me. I am who I am. I would share everything with anyone. I love the lifestyle I live. I wish everybody could live this lifestyle. That is a difficult question and it hurts me that people don't like me because I want everyone to like me.

Your life wasn't always like this.

I come from meager beginnings. I lived in Broadalbin [a rural town 25 miles west of Saratoga Springs]. My mom and dad still live in the same home I was brought up in. My husband came from nothing. We've built everything we have and we share it with the community. It's not like we are selfish. We share.

July 17, 2015
Albany Business Review

*   *   *

I liked this interview because I thought readers got an unvarnished view of a wealthy socialite. Michele Riggi didn't know I was going to print her exact words, her assistant told me afterward, and felt the article was insensitive. But she liked the photo.

An update on her pets: she has 36 dogs and "one cat, two canaries, ten saltwater fish and 15 Koi fish," according to an article in the July 2017 issue of HerLife Magazine.

GEORGE DEUTSCH

President, Advantage Transit Group

George Deutsch was a 25-year-old taxi driver in Budapest, Hungary when he faced a wrenching choice: flee his homeland, leaving behind his wife and 3-year-old son; or face arrest for not snitching on the prostitutes, bellhops and others he knew in the underground world of the Communist regime. His decision started him on a long, vexing road that wound up in Albany, where he now owns a fleet of 40 limousines, party buses and sedans, along with about 25 taxis. The growing business, with about $7 million in annual revenue and more than 100 employees, will have to compete with Uber if the ride-hailing service is allowed to expand upstate. Deutsch isn't terribly concerned.

What was the hardest part for you growing up in a Communist regime?

It was never free. I'm a Jew. My father was [persecuted] during World War II. Some of his family members were taken to Auschwitz. Everyone on my father's side emigrated to Israel but my father stayed behind. He got married, and then I was born.

Driving a taxi was a good job in Budapest. Why did you flee the country?

When you drive a taxi you can either just pick up the calls through the radio or you can have connections to the underground. I had friends who were prostitutes in hotels and it was illegal back then. It's not something the Communist regime would tolerate. The police would come and try to make you work for them, so they could get information, and they let you work. I didn't want to do that.

That must have been very difficult, especially since you were married with a 3-year-old son.

I didn't want to go to jail. If you become a snitch, then you give up the guys you grew up with, and it was not something that I could take.

What did you do?

I went to see the rabbi. I asked him to give me a paper to verify that I'm Jewish-born, and I escaped to Austria. I paid for a tour and got on a bus.

The Hebrew Immigrant Aid Society (HIAS) helped you and other refugees go from Vienna to Rome to New York City.

I was in a cheap Manhattan hotel. I didn't speak much English. We went down in the streets. I had $500 and was robbed. I went to HIAS and they gave me some money, bought me a ticket and sent me to Los Angeles. I worked weekends as a waiter. I cut palm trees. You do anything. I worked for a gentleman who was in real estate, doing drywall.

How did you wind up in Albany?

HIAS was in the process of getting my wife and son out of Hungary. I didn't want to live in New York City. My wife and son came in 1986-87. By then I had an apartment through the Jewish Family Center. They rented an apartment for us in Albany on Lark Street.

George Deutsch, president, Advantage Transit Group.
[Photo by Donna Abbott-Vlahos, courtesy of *Albany Business Review*]

You worked several jobs, including delivering pizza and driving for a cab company. How did you wind up owning a taxi in 1993?

The taxi medallions in Albany were capped. You couldn't apply or buy them. I was playing bridge with a guy who had medallions. He lost, and I won one of his medallions. I took his car and the medallion and went to see a traffic safety officer to make sure it was allowed. We went to Jack Byrne Ford [in Mechanicville] because the car was too old. He was a super guy. I said 'I have no credit, I need a car,' and he made it happen.

You worked for Yellow Cab Co., but were able to buy other medallions?

You had to obey their rules but you could be an independent contractor. Every time someone was selling medallions, I wound up buying them [they could cost about $10,000 each]. You work as much as you can, work 70 to 80 hours per week. Save as much as you can so when an opportunity comes up to buy a medallion, you buy it.

After three generations of running Yellow Cab Co., the Fineman family sold you the business in 2004. How many vehicles did you own?

We had 40 taxis and two limos. I knew the taxi business was something you can't really build on. If anything, the numbers were declining because credit was easier, and people were able to get their own cars.

Do you feel the reputation of Albany cab drivers is deserved or unfair?

It's deserved. Cab driving [in Hungary] is a profession people can be proud of. Over here, it's the last profession anybody wants to do. Taxi drivers are independent contractors. I'm nothing but a car rental company. I have my own detail shop. I have steam-cleaning machines. I used to also pay a lot of money for Colonial Car Wash for any car to go in there. If the cab drivers don't want to take time to do that, I can't force them. Now, because of Uber [possibly coming to Albany], we're having the cars detailed every 15 days.

Cabbies have to deal with bad passengers.

When the college kids are in town, we have a ridiculous number of problems. They throw up in the car, they leave pizza, they disrespect everything. At SUNY, the minute the car stops, [some] run away.

You don't think Uber will succeed in Albany. Why?

Uber is only good if they have drivers. The drivers Uber is going to get are the same drivers we have. If you take my cab today and you have a problem with the driver because the cab is dirty, it's not because of me. If he's going to work under Uber, what is going to change?

January 22, 2016
Albany Business Review

*   *   *

Uber, Lyft and other ride-hailing services became legal throughout New York in June 2017.

One year later, George Deutsch said he had underestimated the competition. He initially lost half his taxi business, he told my colleague, Mike DeSocio.

Deutsch put more effort into other services, such as limousines and medical transports. He said his business had stabilized.

"As scary as it was in the beginning, the popularity it had, I think it leveled out," Deutsch said of Uber and Lyft.

URI KAUFMAN

CEO and president, The Harmony Group

Did you hear the one about the attorney who was fired three times before finding his true calling as a real estate developer? Uri Kaufman can tell you all about it.

What's the most interesting thing growing up the son of a rabbi?

My mom always said that rabbinics is the lowest-paying end of show business.

How did he combine being a father and a rabbi?

Maybe I should lie on the couch. My dad is a great educator. There's a lot of wisdom, what can I say? There was not a lot of sermonizing, not judgmental at all. He's just a very nice guy. Someone who wants to instinctively help someone else.

You were never interested in becoming a rabbi?

No. Everyone in my family is a rabbi. My uncle, my two grandparents, my younger brother, my cousins. The theory in the family is I was switched at birth. Somewhere out there is a short real estate developer with a kid who's a rabbi but he doesn't know why.

Uri Kaufman, CEO, The Harmony Group
[Photo by Donna Abbott-Vlahos, courtesy of *Albany Business Review*]

But seriously folks...

You asked me what it was like growing up the son of a rabbi. It was one one-liner after another.

After graduating from high school in 1982 you studied in Jerusalem for two years, learning Hebrew. When you returned to the U.S. you went to Queens College in New York City at night and worked during the day. What did you do?

I tried a lot of different things. I worked in a mortuary, I helped process the remains. I worked in a carpentry shop basically lifting wood all day. I worked as a waiter. I wrote a novel that was so bad that I just start laughing every time I think about it.

You eventually went to law school at NYU. I understand you had a famous classmate.

John F. Kennedy Jr. Because our last names both begin with the letter 'K' I am right next to him in the picture book. Nobody knows it, but I'm in there.

How well did you get to know him?

I wasn't one of his close friends. He was kind of shy, had a hard time with the girls ... I'm kidding. He was actually a really, really nice guy. Really down to earth, and what happened was a great American tragedy.

Did he handle celebrity well?

Incredibly well. He was the epitome of class. He was named sexiest man alive while we were there. He was just this regular, ordinary person. If you remember he had a hard time passing the bar exam, like many people. He handled it extremely well, with class and dignity.

Did you pass the bar after you graduated in 1989?

I did indeed. On the first try, I might add. And it was all downhill after that.

Why aren't you an attorney today?

It has to do with something my last boss said to me. You're fired.

Why were you fired?

It was a classic case of discrimination. The law firm discriminated against lawyers that were competent and lawyers that weren't.

How long did you last as an attorney?

The longest I ever lasted in a law firm was nine months, counting severance, and I went through three of them as a matter of fact.

I'm still trying to figure out when you're kidding and when you're serious.

I'm dead serious.

You were fired three times?

I was fired three times. I hit the trifecta. It was because I was a really lousy lawyer.

After the third time, did you feel deflated or relieved?

A little of both. I sensed early on this wasn't for me. I lived at the top of a very steep hill. When I got fired the last time, about halfway up the hill I was just thinking, 'You know something. It's a big world and there's a place in it for me.' And that's fine.

How did you become a real estate developer?

It was a very, very good time to be a failed lawyer trying to break into the real estate business. This was July 4, 1992, the S&L crisis. The government bundled all these assets into packages and sold them for whatever they could get. It was a very good time for somebody young with not a whole lot of money to get established.

How did you come up with the $120,000 to make your first investment?

I had to find somebody to put the money up. That's the hardest part of being an entrepreneur.

Did you buy more distressed properties?

Absolutely. I have a $10,000-a-day real estate habit to support. That business ended in late '95, and then I had to go out and become a real estate developer.

The key was buying these things cheap. We managed to find cheap properties and develop them and turn them around.

How did you get interested in the old Harmony Mills in Cohoes?

We saw it advertised. But what really attracted me to Cohoes was the people, starting with Mayor McDonald, without whom we'd be nothing but a pile of bricks.

What was your reaction when you saw the building in person the first time?

I was bowled over. It's a spectacular building.

Did this project make you want to do more like it?

Absolutely. This is a business that lets you feel good about yourself. It takes a lot of patience, a lot of determination. I often say this is the opposite of day trading. It takes years and years before you can turn something like this around.

September 27, 2010
Albany Business Review

*   *   *

Uri Kaufman rescued two relics of the region's industrial past by converting huge, empty manufacturing buildings into 485 apartments. Harmony Mills in Cohoes and Albany International in Menands are now full of tenants.

Other deals he has pursued fell apart for various reasons.

I called him in September 2018 to ask if he's still passionate about real estate investing.

"Yes, but I'm just a little burned out," he said. "It's a tough business because so many things can go wrong. They really aren't your fault but they just happen and someone has to be responsible and that's me."

He said his proudest accomplishment was renovating Harmony Mills, a sprawling former textile mill built in the mid-1800s along the Mohawk River.

A couple days later he sent me this email: "I've been thinking a lot about our conversation. You asked me what I'm proudest of. The truth is, it's not Albany International. It's not even Harmony. It's this: In my 26 years doing this, I've probably borrowed over $200 million. I have paid back every penny on time. The banks know this. That's why they lend me more. Good ethics really is good business."

AFRIM NEZAJ

Owner, Afrim's Sports

Afrim Nezaj was born in Kosovë in the former Yugoslavia and came to America with his family at age 10. Over the past 33 years he's built a small empire, becoming the go-to guy for youths and adults who want to play soccer, flag football or lacrosse in the middle of winter — or any other time of the year.

What was it like coming to America and living with 15 family members in a small Bronx apartment?

It was normal because I always shared a bed with my brothers, but this one had heat, lights 24 hours a day, and a fridge. We were coming from a pretty poor background, but we never knew we were poor.

You played soccer at University of Albany, but also had a side job.

I was a building superintendent [at the university] when all the staff left. I would always try to play as much soccer as I could in the school gyms, but it was really hard to get playing time. I thought, why don't I get my friends to chip in and go play [at the Washington Avenue Armory]? We were paying the guard there. I was still not an entrepreneur. I just wanted to play.

Afrim Nezaj, owner, Afrim's Sports.
[Photo by Donna Abbott-Vlahos, courtesy of *Albany Business Review*]

That set the ball in motion toward eventually starting an indoor soccer business at the armory. Having children was another turning point.

There was a time a friend of mine was asking me for a discount. My daughter was 3 years old. I said, 'Honey, come over here. Honey, you know the coat daddy was going to buy you for Christmas? I may not be able to buy it because he wants a discount.' The guy looks at me and says, 'What's wrong with you?' I said that's what you're asking me to do. If I don't collect that money, she won't get a coat. From then on, I was a little more disciplined in everything I did.

You had a lot of help from Harry Apkarian and other Schenectady leaders when you started hosting indoor soccer games at the old Center City downtown.

I'm sitting with these four guys at a diner. They said, 'Young man, we have to do our due diligence. Do you have a P and L [profit and loss statement]? Do you know what a P and L is?' I said no, but I'll learn. That's how weak I was. But these guys invested in me.

Your dad loaned you the money so you could buy the indoor facility on Albany Shaker Road in Colonie.

My dad was in New York City getting older, and tired of running apartments. He says take all the money, put it in the building [in Colonie] and just give me what I need to live off each year. As long as he lives, I will give him that. That's his security. I got the money to do what I want, and he gets what he needs.

You've had to overcome a lot of obstacles in your life. How confident are you town officials will approve your new soccer dome?

I'm one of those people that if I was running and I had a 10-yard lead, I'd think I had a 5-yard lead. I always respect the opposition. If you ask my confidence level, I don't know. There are so many unknowns here.

What's your best advice for someone who wants to start and build a successful business?

I found if I satisfy enough people, they are going to help me. Find out what people want. Ask them. And then, they give me money. Isn't that great? They allow me to support my family, to travel. I've visited 42 countries. There's another 100 I want to visit.

October 18, 2013
Albany Business Review

*   *   *

Around the time this interview was published, Afrim Nezaj wanted to build another indoor, multi-purpose sports dome in Colonie, this time with four adjacent outdoor fields.

There was so much demand from athletic leagues he knew an expansion was needed.

He estimated the cost at $6 million to $8 million.

He got the approvals he needed from the town. Little did he realize it would take nearly five years to break ground and the cost would balloon to $13 million.

The old farmland is near a large cemetery and other property being developed into apartments — two factors that contributed to the long municipal approval process and higher costs.

When I called him in September 2018 to get an update on the construction, I asked about the delays he encountered.

"Someone said you just want it so bad because anyone else who had these kind of delays would have said it's not worth doing," he told me.

He's excited about the new facilities, and expects to open around Thanksgiving.

"It's turning out better than I thought," he said.

SUSAN NOVOTNY

Owner, The Book House of Stuyvesant Plaza, Market Block Books

Susan Novotny is one of those rare people who have combined their passion with their profession.

Do you remember the first book you ever read, or that was read to you?

It would have to have been a large collection of the original Golden Books. I can remember pretty clearly the Poky Little Puppy [and] Tootle. I remember Rudyard Kipling's books in the Golden Book form.

Your mother was a registered nurse and a bookworm. Was it pre-ordained that you would love reading too?

She would always have her nose in a book. When you're raised in that environment, you just learn at a very early age that's entertainment.

Do you ever long for the days growing up in a small town in the early '50s?

Absolutely. All the time. When we had a couple of days this winter when the snow was just a little too heavy to open the store, I thought, 'Gosh, this is heaven.' I can't get to work. I don't have to worry about work because the other people aren't there either. I get to just stay home and catch up on my reading.

Do you like to write in your spare time?

No. I'm not one of these people who feels I have the great American novel trying to claw its way out of my soul. I'm more than content to appreciate the efforts of other people.

You spent 10 years as a saleswoman in the publishing industry. What did you learn?

I learned the publishing industry from the ground up — how a book is found through an agent or from an author; the profit-and-loss statement that you do on each one; how much you are going to pay in royalties to this author; and how much of an advance you are going to give them; how many copies do you need to print; how many do you absolutely, positively need to sell to make back the advance, and how many more do you need to sell on top of it to make a profit.

Your first son, Alexander, was born in 1984. How did that change your professional life?

Trying to breastfeed and sell books on the road just doesn't work out. One day I pulled over, called my boss and I said 'I'm sorry but I think I'm needed more at home than out here in the field.' I left gracefully.

Let's do some word association. What's the first thing that comes to your mind when I say Barnes & Noble?

Oh my goodness. It can't be printed, it can't be printed.

Amazon?

Blood-sucking thieves.

Kindle?

Potential.

Susan Novotny, owner,
The Book House of Stuyvesant Plaza and Market Block Books.
[Photo by Donna Abbott-Vlahos, courtesy of *Albany Business Review*]

How do you feel about digital books?

I know a number of people who use the Sony Reader, which is the competitive model to the Kindle. For reading academic, scholarly, technical or professional books, it makes perfect sense. If you're an editor in New York and just received an e-manuscript from one of your authors and you want to sit on the subway and correct pages, it's perfect. But when it comes time to actually sit down with a good 400-page novel or history book or biography, nothing beats the smell of the book, the crack of the spine, the turn of the pages, and the general sensory experience that you cannot get with the Sony Reader or the Kindle.

Do you know who you are going to support in the presidential election?

Yes, I think I do.

Are you willing to say?

I'm going to vote for McCain.

You realize you're defying a stereotype. You're a female owner of a bookstore. Most people would probably think you're a Democrat and you would support Hillary.

I'm really sick of right-wing conservatism and I'm sick of knee-jerk liberals, too. I've had it with both ends of the spectrum. I'm of the feeling this country's hope really rests on people who can remain independent of either party and make clear judgments based on the person and the policies they propose and their integrity. I might change my mind. McCain might turn out to be a buffoon. Who knows? Whoever could run my bookstore is who I'll ultimately vote for.

June 9, 2008
Albany Business Review

*   *   *

Susan Novotny is still selling books, but competition from Amazon — along with a decline in book readership — forced her to reduce the size of her store and staff at Stuyvesant Plaza.

She wouldn't be in business were it not for her helpful landlord [The Swyer Cos.] and her husband's financial support.

"There's no money in this business anymore," Novotny said during a panel discussion about retail hosted by the Albany Business Review in May 2018.

The constant battle had worn her down by 2017 and she was ready to give up. But a conversation with her son, Alexander, who was working for a literary agent in Las Vegas, changed her mind.

"He said, 'Oh no, mom. I'll come back.' He's stepped into the line of succession."

MARV

REMEMBERING A GREAT
REPORTER AND GREAT FRIEND

December 7, 2016

Albany Business Review

Marv Cermak and I used to joke nobody dies in obituaries anymore. They just pass away.

"Pass away" is one of those euphemisms Cermak hated, so let's say it like it is: Cermak, a longtime reporter and columnist at *The Times Union*, died Tuesday morning at age 84.

I'm going to miss him very much.

He was a great friend and mentor for most of the 25 years I've been a reporter.

The news business, like all businesses, is high-pressure. Reporters are constantly trying to get the story first.

One of the best things I learned from Cermak was you could be friendly with the competition and still do your job well. They aren't the enemy.

Cermak demonstrated this time and again when I was the new kid on the block covering Schenectady City Hall during my previous job at *The Daily Gazette*.

Here was a guy with decades of experience and countless sources, whose home in the Mont Pleasant neighborhood was the de facto Schenectady bureau of *The Times Union*.

His wife, Patty, would answer the phone, day or night, "Hello, *Times Union*," and take his messages.

Cermak beat me on plenty of stories, but didn't lord it over me. He knew what it was like to be on the receiving end, and would often say he was up against seven reporters covering Schenectady County alone.

We would sometimes scribble messages to each other on our reporter notebooks during city council meetings, stunned or amused by what we were witnessing. A sense of humor goes a long way in this job, and he made me laugh a lot.

He was one-of-a-kind in many ways. His daily routine was a vestige from his days at the former *Knickerbocker News*, an afternoon paper with early-morning deadlines. He went to sleep around sunrise, and woke up in the afternoon.

Insomniacs always knew they could call the house at 2 a.m. and he'd be wide awake to talk.

His ability to recall names, dates, places and other specific details from long ago floored me. Stories flowed out of him like an open spigot.

He was born March 7, 1932, in Schenectady. His parents, Joseph and Beatrice, were both deaf. His mother lost her hearing from scarlet fever; his father, from diphtheria. Marv was their only surviving son. Another boy died from tonsillitis before Marv was born. Those were the days before antibiotics could treat that sort of ailment.

"I was a loner because my parents couldn't hear," he told me once. "I went to the streets because there was no TV, there was very little radio, so I heard no voices. I hit the street to communicate and hear people talk."

His dad worked in a part of the huge General Electric plant that made insulators. It was tough, grueling work but jobs were plentiful back then. Marv also worked there a couple of years as a payroll clerk in the turbine division before he was drafted by the Army for the Korean War.

A neighbor who was a local Republican committeeman tried to arrange for Marv to get a deferment because both his parents were deaf.

"All my buddies were getting drafted," he told me. "I said I can't take that deferment because I knew my mother and father could live on their own."

He returned home three years later and planned to resume working at GE, but his boss wouldn't take him back because he wanted Marv to go to college on the G.I. Bill. So he went to the old Albany Business College and learned bookkeeping and accounting.

He also got a part-time job at the *Gazette* in Schenectady, ripping stories off the teletype machines every 15 minutes and sending them down a chute to the city desk. The wire room, as it was called, was next to the sports department.

When the sports staff was short-handed, they'd ask Marv to answer the phones and write down the box scores that were called in by high school coaches.

"One time, I remember I handed notes from a JV football game or something like that to a sportswriter and he said 'don't give it to me.' He says 'write it.' I said 'what do you mean write it?' I said 'I don't know how to write.' He said, 'Well, how do you know you don't know how to write? You never tried.' I said 'all right.' I wrote this little JV story. He looked at it, went over the thing with his pencil. It was maybe four or five paragraphs. He said you 'misspelled a word or something. It's fine.' And I said, 'you're kidding.'"

That's how he got started in the newspaper business. From the Gazette he went to the *Knickerbocker News* in 1969 and then *The Times Union* after the Knick folded.

He retired as a reporter in 2002, but continued writing a weekly column, "Covering Schenectady."

Fittingly, his last column ran Tuesday, the day he died.

What made him such a great reporter was his determination, honesty, curiosity and fearlessness. If the truth hurt, so be it.

Humility was also central to his character. He knew his flaws, and didn't act like he was better than anyone else. He could be cranky and gruff.

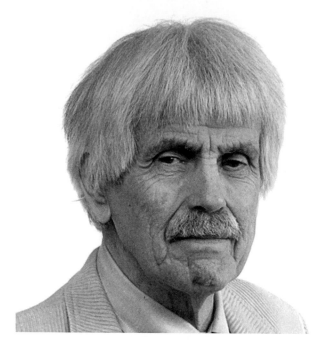

Marv Cermak
[Photo by Luanne M. Ferris, courtesy of *The Times Union*]

But he would also go out of his way to help someone in need. He was often among the first people who friends called with the news that their mother or father died. He had a sympathetic ear and big heart.

The last thing he would have wanted in death was people fawning over him, writing "puff pieces and all that crap."

Sorry, Marv.

Over the years we became closer and shared much about our lives. He never betrayed a confidence. I had complete trust in him.

If any death can be called bittersweet, his certainly qualifies.

He suffered terrible pain after falling off a stool in his Schenectady home five years ago and damaging his spine. Patty's death in January 2015 added to his agony, compounded by loneliness.

He considered himself a prisoner in his own home, a terrible fate for someone accustomed to always being on the go.

"People jump out of airplanes and walk away fine," he would say ruefully. "I fell three feet and wind up a cripple."

Toward the end, his hands were so gnarled he would type with one finger, yet continued cranking out weekly columns. Phone calls and regular visits from friends kept him in the loop.

We knew he longed for his suffering to be over. The moment finally came.

Selfishly, I wish we could have had a little more time together.

*   *   *

A little over a month after Marv died, the union that represents editorial and advertising staff at The Times Union announced it received a $50,000 bequest from Marv, the single largest donation in the union's long history.

The Guild decided to create The Cermak Award, which consists of two, $1,000 awards annually for union members who do outstanding work.

I'm sure Marv would be happy to know how the money will be spent.

On a sad note, it wasn't mentioned in my story but Marv and Patty had one child, Michael. They were estranged for a long time. I didn't ask Marv many questions about what happened because I knew it was a painful subject, but he would occasionally talk about it.

I know Marv tried to help his son, but Michael lived a tough adult life, unable to support himself. I never met Michael, nor did I seek him out after Marv died. I wish I had.

Michael died on February 19, 2018. He was 56.

THANK YOU

My mom and dad, Maria and John DeMasi, left behind their family, friends and all that was familiar for better opportunities in America. Their hard work and sacrifice made my path much easier, including the decision to become a journalist. I also benefited from being the youngest of four children. My siblings Ralph, Nell and Judy helped raise me, and I learned a lot from their experiences.

I had been a reporter for eight years when Lori and I were married in 2000. I couldn't have continued in the job without her love and support. During our early years together she had to contend with my unpredictable schedule. Then, after our children were born, many nights when I had work to do at home.

Balancing family and job responsibilities is a constant struggle for parents. Our burden has been greatly lifted by my father-in-law, Tom Mithen, who is always there for us, and my brother-in-law, Dave Mithen, who loves our children as if they were his own.

Over the years I've read a few collections of newspaper stories but didn't think it was something I could do until coming across one published by Dave Blow, who I worked with at *The Post-Star*. His book opened my eyes to the possibility and his advice helped me pursue the idea.

One of my first steps was getting permission to republish the stories and photos. A 'no' from any of the three papers would have doomed my plan. Saying 'yes' were Ken Tingley at *The Post-Star*; Judy Patrick and Miles Reed at *The Daily Gazette*; Cindy Applebaum, Mike Hendricks, Joanne Skoog and Ashley Ganci at the *Albany Business Review*/American City Business Journals.

I knew I needed an editor for this book, someone I could trust to devote the time to reading every word and not be afraid to tell me what I needed to hear. It had to be someone with a passion for storytelling, an eye for detail, and a drive to get the work done on their personal time. I found that person sitting next to me in the office: Mike DeSocio, digital editor at the *Albany Business Review*. It was a joy working with him. Mike's talents go well beyond editing. He also designed the front and back covers, both of which were given a 'nip-and-tuck' at home by Melissa Mangini, managing editor.

Newspaper archival systems are periodically updated. Old stories and photos are sometimes lost or purged. Those are two reasons why it was so difficult to find some material. Bob Condon at *The Post-Star* went to great lengths to find articles and photos I needed. Jeff Wilkin and Jeff Haff at *The Daily Gazette* also went above and beyond to track down photos I requested.

One of my great pleasures as a reporter has been working with talented photographers. The images taken by five of them are featured in these pages: Monty Calvert, Meredith Kaiser, Hans Pennink, Marc Schultz and Donna Abbott-Vlahos.

A first-time book author has lots of questions for the publisher. So many, it would be understandable if their incoming emails were eventually blocked. That never happened at The Troy Book Makers. Madison Feldhaus, a graphic designer, kept hitting the reply button, and kept me going. Manager Jessika Hazelton took on the project at a critical time after Feldhaus left the publishing company. She quickly relieved my anxiety over the transition, and her deft touch made the layout sparkle.

Andrew Roiter, digital producer at *Albany Business Review*, didn't hesitate when I sought his skills to help me market this book online on his personal time.

I've drawn inspiration from many sources during my career, but two stand out: my high school journalism teacher, Mrs. Coyle, who saw in me something I didn't know existed; and Marv Cermak, whose honesty, work ethic and humor were a model for me.

I have worked with many editors who taught me how to be a better reporter: Sue Graves at *The Spotlight*; Steve Bennett, Tamara Dietrich, Mark Mahoney, Will Doolittle and Bob Condon at *The Post-Star*; George Walsh, Mal Provost and Maggie Hartley at *The Daily Gazette*; and Mike Hendricks at the *Albany Business Review*.

Two former colleagues were instrumental in advancing my career. Shirin Parsavand put the good word in for me after she left *The Post-Star* to work at *The Daily Gazette*. I eventually followed her there. Rick D'Errico laid the groundwork for my move from the *Gazette* to the *Albany Business Review*.

The student paper at Ithaca College has won many awards over the years, but it wasn't held in high regard during my first two years at school. That changed in my junior year when Paul Heaton became student advisor at *The Ithacan*. He's no longer there, but he had a big impact on me and the paper.

I've worked with many talented, dedicated reporters and page designers during my career — too numerous to list. There were other journalists whose work I admired from afar.

Reporters can't do their job unless people — many of them strangers — are willing to tell their story. These conversations often happen at a single point in time. Occasionally they continue over months or years and a working relationship is formed based on trust and mutual respect. I've been fortunate to experience both in my career.

I've been blessed in many ways: my family, my health and my job. I'm grateful to God for all that I have.